Praise for

"One of the best organized, most vivid, lively and informative books I've ever seen. Nothing outshines the mind of an engineer who has an imaginative religious faith and a lucid pen… I hope **frameworks** takes the nation by storm."

—**Tom McBride** College English professor, author

"Jesus says that his parables are for 'those who have ears to hear.' **frameworks** helps us get our ears on." —**Dave Olson** Professional truck driver

"Fresh, innovative and extremely unique. A fabulous resource for boosting biblical literacy dramatically, both among Christ followers in our congregation and across the Western world."

—**Steve Madsen** Lead pastor, Cornerstone Fellowship

"**frameworks** goes beyond academia to practical applications. If I were to teach a New Testament Survey class, I would use this book."

—**Ada Lum** Teacher of Bible teachers in 115 countries

"Hefty, gorgeous and breathtaking. This is National Geographic in a book. It makes you want to sit down and read it… and then leave it out on your coffee table." —**Dave Mosby** Former software CEO, author

"A delicious book… simple, but substantive. Help. I'm addicted… I can't put it down." —**Doug Stevens** Men's ministry leader

"Eric Larson's new book is delightful. With an approachable style, vivid illustrations and fascinating stories, Eric makes the New Testament landscape easy to traverse, even for novice explorers."

—**Penny Warner** Educator, author of parenting books

"Eric is the most engaging Bible teacher I have ever met. What an awesome book."

—**Steve Patterson** Oakland Athletics usher supervisor

"Even after studying the Bible for over 28 years, I learn something new on every page. **frameworks** refreshes my love for the Bible and gives me new tools for sharing it with others".

—**Lanette Smith** Art teacher, blogger, lover of words

"I like this book. I *really, really* like this book."

—**Marilyn Miller** Womens' Bible study teacher, author

"As one of those people who panicked when asked to 'open your Bible to…,' I now feel confident that I can find my way. **frameworks** has taken the intimidation factor out of the New Testament for me."

—**Carole Johnson** Former school administrator

"Superbly crafted and exceedingly helpful. **frameworks** will help you navigate your way through the twists and turns of the New Testament text."

—**Phil Comfort** Editor, Bible scholar, author

"I used **frameworks** to tour the entire New Testament with my fourth graders this year. They loved it, and I did too."

—**Deb Stoner** Elementary school teacher

"**frameworks** helped me learn about Paul's letters. I noticed that he starts every one with 'Grace and peace to you.'"

—**Nia Karnes** Fourth grader (grinning from ear to ear)

"An excellent way to structure the New Testament in your mind. I can envision churches all over the country using **frameworks** in small groups to eat up the Bible."　—**Rachel Karpanty-Yantis** Marketing director

"This is the best Bible study I've seen in years. It's like tasting something wonderful… you just want to taste more. **frameworks** excites people to go deeper."　—**Stan Johnson** Retired pastor

"Eric's writing pulls you in. You don't feel like you're 'learning,' but that you're getting to know someone better."　—**Jennie Reeb** College student

"I am totally digging **frameworks**. An incredible resource. A killer book."　—**Shiloh Hagen** Real estate professional

"Eric has successfully captured everything that we love about his classes, especially his funky drawings, sense of humor and unbridled enthusiasm for all things God."　—**Fred & Tamy Shaw** Business people, Bible study lovers

"This book is phenomenal. Besides being gorgeous to look at, it's an absolute treasure trove of New Testament details in bite-sized pieces."　—**Chris Nunn** Printed-circuit board designer

"A great read. Thoughtful and organized. The Indy 500 of New Testament Surveys. A real checkered flag winner."　—**Barry Bronson** Writer, former auto racing executive

frameworks™

4 1 9 4 8 1

How to Navigate the New Testament

An Extraordinary Guide for Ordinary People

Eric Larson

Frameworks Resources LLC

frameworks
How to Navigate the New Testament
An Extraordinary Guide for Ordinary People
by Eric Larson

Published by Frameworks Resources LLC
1005 Dunhill Court, Danville, CA 94506
eric@frameworksthebook.com
www.frameworksthebook.com

Art Direction, Book Design & Production, and Cover Art
Bridget Whitaker, Along the Road Arts, (925) 321-1537
alongtheroad@comcast.net
www.alongtheroadarts.com

Book Production and Printing
Chromagraphics, (925) 484-1141
ron@chromaprinting.com
www.chromaprinting.com

ISBN 978-0-615-63312-1

First printing, 2012
Second printing, 2013

Printed in the United States of America

To my wife, Bonnie.
Thank you for your constant partnership,
your unwavering support, and for
giving me space to fiddle endlessly with words.
You're a doll, Sweets. Love you.
This one's for you.

Table of Contents

Introduction

Here's a story I hear a lot. You're visiting a new church or attending the one you call home, when the pastor asks everyone to grab a Bible, open it up—"Please turn to Matthew chapter 25, verse 14"—and read along with him. On the back of the cushy auditorium chair directly in front of you, you see a spiffy red Bible that some wonderfully efficient staff person has placed there, correctly anticipating your current need.

Instinctively, you reach for it and crack it open. Problem is, you don't have the slightest clue where Matthew is or how on God's green earth you'll ever find chapter 25 in time, much less verse 14. As you begin to fumble your way through a few pages, searching in vain for Matthew, your eyes glance to your left where you notice that your neighbor is already safely home in Matthew and, smiling confidently, ready to read.

A few butterflies begin to flutter in your stomach as you contemplate your next move. At that moment, you have two options: 1) fake it—put your thumbs squarely over the word *Habbakuk* in the upper right and left hand corners of the pages you just opened to, smile and pretend that everything is okay; or 2) turn to that smug-looking person on your left and say, "Excuse me—but where exactly *is* Matthew?" If this is you—you've come to the right place.

If that hasn't been your experience, maybe this is you. You live at the other end of the biblical food chain, having read your Bible faithfully since the time you were in kindergarten. Over the years you've memorized dozens of verses, attended countless studies and have walked through the Scriptural forest so many times that they've named paths after you.

One day, you're enjoying a cup of coffee with friends who, with your help, are reading the Bible for the first time. Suddenly, they look at you rather quizzically (O thou fount of all wisdom) and from nowhere blurt out: "We were just wondering, why does the New Testament start with Matthew? And why are some books soooo long and others so short? And why do most of the books have such peculiar names? We don't get it. It's all so confusing."

(Hmm... you mutter to yourself—good questions—I wish I knew.)

A few butterflies begin to flutter in your stomach as you contemplate your next move. At that moment, you have two options: 1) fake it—lean forward, strike a confident pose and make up some fancy story on the fly. "Well... you see... um... a long time ago... ahh... right after Jesus ascended to heaven...," or 2) simply look at them and say, "You know what? I have *no* idea. But I'm sure we can find out." If this is you—you've also come to the right place.

Navigation and context

These stories highlight two real challenges many people face when they open their Bibles: navigation and context. Navigation is the ability to weave your way among the Bible's 66 books (and 1,189 chapters) without getting lost—to know where you are now and how to safely travel to where you want to go.

At the individual book level, navigation can be thought of as knowing how the book of the Bible that you're currently reading is organized and what landmarks you should watch for to guide you through it. In the "You can't see the forest for the trees" metaphor, navigation is all about the trees.

Context, on the other hand, looks squarely at the forest, helping you see the big picture to discover how the trees fit together. Whereas navigation asks where and how questions, context asks who, what, when and why.

I recently taught an eight-week course for newer Bible readers at a large church not far from where I live. It was your typical "Survey of the New Testament" class that I had taught for a few years. But this time, to be a bit more cool, hip and trendy, we decided to advertise it with a catchy title, "Building Your Bible Skills—How to Navigate the Entire New Testament."

At the first class session, as I glanced around the room to see who had registered, I was shocked to see a member of the church's Elder Board, sitting in the front row. Fred, as we'll call him for now, had been a serious Bible student for years. "Why in the world did you sign up for this class?" I asked him. "Well," he replied, "though I've studied the books of the New Testament individually, I've never seen how they all fit together. That's why I'm here."

Maybe that's why you're here too.

Why Frameworks?

frameworks, quite simply, is a book about Bible navigation and context—material that's designed to build your confidence in your ability to negotiate the text and understand it. Think of it as a guidebook, a Bible companion, written for anyone who would like to have a personal biblical tour guide. This book can be used for self-study, in small group discussions or in classrooms to set the context for Bible reading and to lead you through it.

Since the Bible is so large, this volume of **frameworks** covers only the New Testament, the 27 books that begin with the birth of Christ.

Also, since most of us are visual learners, **frameworks** is a visual book that presents ideas and concepts through pictures, in addition to written words. Its compelling stories, embedded maps and color photos work hand-in-hand to build striking mental images—unforgettable impressions that aid understanding.

These images become the conceptual frameworks that connect the new things you're learning with things you already know and help you organize it all. Think of them as structures upon which you can hang your thoughts. Just like the steel girders that hold up skyscrapers, or the wooden beams that frame houses, your mind needs frameworks to make sense of what you read.

Thus, the title of the book—**frameworks**.

Less is more

One more thing before you dive in. These days, since most of us are being buried under avalanches of new information, the last thing we need is another snowstorm. For this reason, we've designed **frameworks** in a simple, clear and easy-to-understand format (with lots of refreshing white space), giving you most of what you need to know without overwhelming you. You are then encouraged to launch out and explore the New Testament on your own.

How Frameworks is Organized

Part 1—New Testament Frameworks

For ease of use, we've separated **frameworks**' contents into two parts. Part One introduces the New Testament as a whole by first walking you through the story of Jesus' life and then providing you with the context into which his story fits.

Here you'll journey with Jesus, mapping his travel through five regions over seven time periods. You'll be learning, as you go, about some of the places he visited and the things he did. Then, after a brief introduction to the larger Roman world, you'll learn about the New Testament's origin and discover why its 27 books are arranged in six groups (notice the **frameworks** logo?).

Finally, you'll meet the eight New Testament writers and look at side-by-side comparisons of their writings to see why the books were placed in their current order.

Part 2—Book Frameworks and Themes

Part Two then takes you on spectacular guided tours of the New Testament's books, one by one. As you tour, you'll gain a foundational understanding of each book as we answer these 10 questions:

1. Intro—What is this book like?
2. Theme—What is this book about?
3. Purpose—Why was it written?
4. Outline—How is the book organized?
5. Verses—How does it read?
6. Navigation—How do I move through it?
7. Unique things—What makes the book or its author special?
8. Recap—What should I remember most?
9. Questions—How can I explore further or go deeper?
10. Insights—What one verse can I apply right now?

Now you're ready. Enjoy your journey.

New Testament Frameworks
Part 1

Where Jesus Walked

Map of Palestine and Surrounds

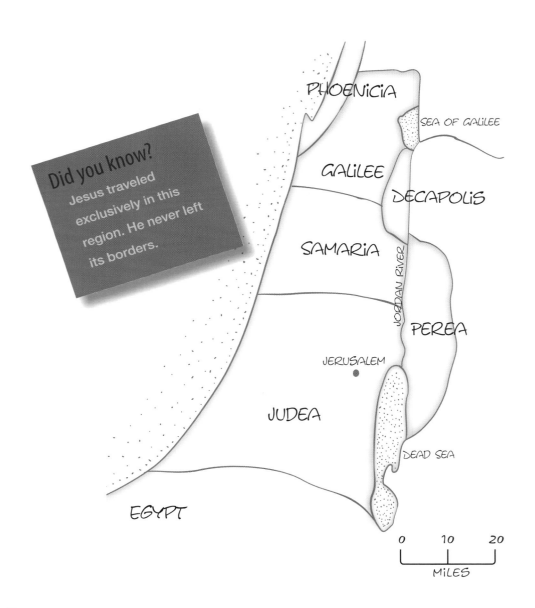

Did you know?
Jesus traveled exclusively in this region. He never left its borders.

PHOENICIA

SEA OF GALILEE

GALILEE

DECAPOLIS

SAMARIA

JORDAN RIVER

PEREA

JERUSALEM

JUDEA

DEAD SEA

EGYPT

0   10   20

MILES

Where Jesus Walked

We're now ready to start our journey with Jesus. (Turn to the map on page 38 to see Palestine in a regional context.) All four Gospels intensively report on this place of Jesus' life's work. Except for a short stay in Egypt following his birth, and a trip or two through Phoenicia, there were only five places on the planet where Jesus walked. Here they are:

Galilee

In the north was *Galilee of the Gentiles*, the place where Jesus spent all of his youth and most of his life. One part of Galilee was mountainous, the other part, fertile plains. At Jesus' time, about two million people lived here, including pockets of cutthroat, Jewish revolutionaries.

Samaria

Sandwiched between Galilee and Judea was Samaria, a rambling, hilly territory that Jewish people avoided like the plague due to the intense hatred that had raged between the Jews and the Samaritans for centuries. When traveling from Galilee to Judea, most Jews would intentionally go around Samaria.

Judea

In the south of Palestine was Judea, the largest of all of the territories and home to Jerusalem, the Holy City with its Holy Temple. Most of Jesus' serious clashes with Jewish religious leaders happened here. While Galilee was green and lush, most of southern Judea was a parched, God-forsaken desert.

Perea

To the east of Judea and Samaria was a small territory across the Jordan River whose name appears nowhere in the Bible. Perea, better known as *beyond the Jordan*, was the place where Jesus was baptized when his ministry began and where he ended his ministry before his crucifixion.

The Decapolis

East of Galilee and Samaria was the Decapolis, a region named for ten Greek cities (*deca* ten, *polis* city). Jesus made this area famous when, during a visit, he cast demons out of a man, into a herd of swine. Now crazed, the hogs ran headlong off a cliff, into the sea. The hog owners politely asked Jesus to leave.

Navigating Jesus' Ministry

Jesus lived on earth for 33½ years. His ministry took place during the last 3½ years of his life. It is helpful to think of Jesus' life in seven distinct phases:

1. **Birth and youth**

   Jesus' first 30 years. The formative time between his birth and his ministry. Here Jesus grows in wisdom and stature and favor with God and man.

2. **Ministry year one**

   The first year of Christ's public ministry. He works his first miracles, attracts his first disciples and introduces people to the kingdom of God.

3. **Ministry in Galilee**

   Jesus stays put in Galilee for 18 months. There he preaches his famous *Sermon on the Mount* and picks twelve "apostles" for further training.

4. **Training the twelve**

   For six months Jesus trains *the twelve*. They watch him work miracles, listen to his teachings and argue with each other about who's the greatest.

5. **Road trip**

   Jesus makes a final swing through Palestine, preaching, teaching and healing. At the end of this trip, Jesus raises Lazarus from the dead.

6. **Passion week**

   This is the last seven days between Jesus' arrival in Jerusalem and his resurrection. It is intensely reported on in all the Gospels.

7. **Resurrection**

   Jesus stays on earth 40 days after his resurrection to wean people away from depending on him physically. Now he'll be spiritually present instead.

Navigating Jesus' Ministry

The six boxes below visually illustrate Jesus' three and a half year ministry broken down into six time periods. The first four of these periods are in months, his Passion lasts one week and his resurrection lasts 40 days.

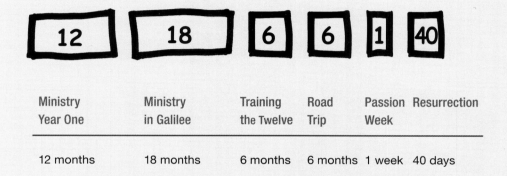

Ministry Year One	Ministry in Galilee	Training the Twelve	Road Trip	Passion Week	Resurrection
12 months	18 months	6 months	6 months	1 week	40 days

Navigating Jesus' Ministry

1. Birth and Youth

Elapsed Time   30 years (4 BC to AD 26)
Places   Bethlehem, Egypt and Nazareth

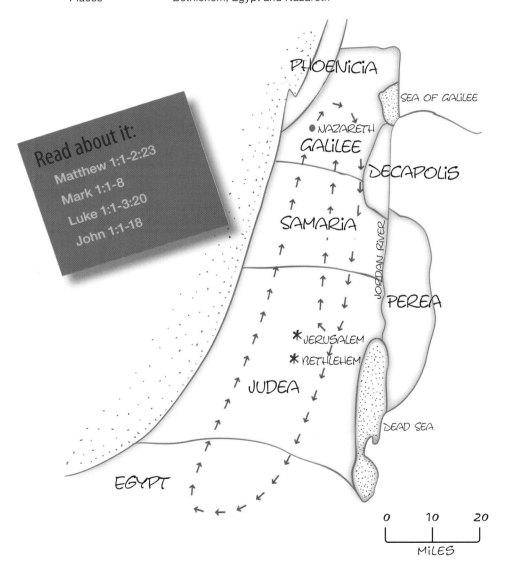

Read about it:
Matthew 1:1-2:23
Mark 1:1-8
Luke 1:1-3:20
John 1:1-18

PHOENICIA

SEA OF GALILEE

NAZARETH

GALILEE

DECAPOLIS

SAMARIA

JORDAN RIVER

PEREA

JERUSALEM

BETHLEHEM

JUDEA

DEAD SEA

EGYPT

0   10   20

MILES

Highlights

Birth and Youth

Jesus is born in the little town of Bethlehem in 4 BC. Sometime after his birth, his father Joseph is warned by an angel of a plot by the evil King Herod to murder Jesus and all the other little baby boys in metro Jerusalem. Herod had heard from wise men that one of these babies would become the *King of the Jews*, and he loathed competition. So Joseph, Mary, and Jesus pack up, head out of town and flee to safety in Egypt.

Some months, or even years, later—no one really knows for sure—Herod dies (good riddance). Another angel soon arrives to inform Joseph that the coast is clear. Joseph now has a green light to return to Palestine, but is strongly urged to bypass toxic Judea. He decides, wisely, to relocate the family up north in Nazareth, where Jesus grows up.

When he is old enough to swing a hammer, Jesus learns his father's trade, as all young Jewish boys do. Though the locals call Jesus *the son of a carpenter*, he and his dad are probably also stonemasons since there are few trees for miles in any direction to cut down and make into furniture or buildings.

It's entirely possible that Joseph and Jesus find steady work in Sepphoris, a Greek city, which, at the time, is being built from the ground up just five miles up the road.

In their biographies of the life of Christ, Matthew and Mark mention that Jesus has four half-brothers—James, Joseph, Jude and Simon—and at least two sisters. That makes seven kids growing up under one "stick and earthen" roof. John adds that during these formative years, none of his brothers believe that Jesus is the Son of God—at least not yet.

Luke says that when Jesus is 12, his parents take him on a road trip to attend a feast at Jerusalem, where they lose track of him for three full days. But, besides these few sketchy details, the Bible reveals precious little about what happens during the first 30 years of Jesus' life.

Navigating Jesus' Ministry

2. Ministry Year One

Elapsed Time   12 months (AD 26-27)
Places   Judea, Perea, Samaria, Galilee
and the Decapolis

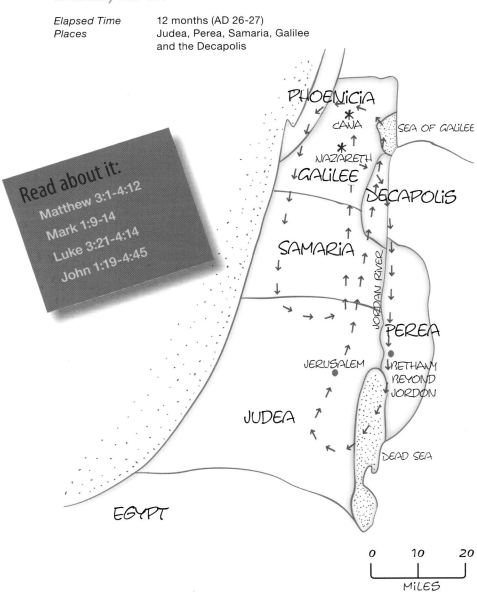

Read about it:
Matthew 3:1-4:12
Mark 1:9-14
Luke 3:21-4:14
John 1:19-4:45

PHOENICIA

*CANA

SEA OF GALILEE

*NAZARETH

GALILEE

DECAPOLIS

SAMARIA

JORDAN RIVER

PEREA

JERUSALEM

BETHANY
BEYOND
JORDON

JUDEA

DEAD SEA

EGYPT

0   10   20

MILES

Highlights

Ministry Year One

At age 30, Jesus says goodbye to friends and family and heads out to begin his life's work. He travels southeast from Nazareth until he arrives a few days later at a place called Bethany Beyond Jordan in Perea. There, he finds his older cousin, John the Baptist, dunking people in the Jordan River and asks John to baptize him too. John complies.

As Jesus comes up out of the water, the Spirit of God, which looks like a dove, descends upon him. The Spirit then leads Jesus southwest into the wilderness of Judea where he fasts for 40 days and overcomes the devil's temptations three times.

Having been anointed by God through baptism and tested by the devil in the desert, Jesus is now duly qualified to proclaim the arrival of God's kingdom on earth.

During the next year, he does just that, traveling on foot from Judea through the districts of Samaria, Decapolis and Galilee, teaching the people, healing the sick, performing miracles and picking up disciples along the way. After successfully crisscrossing the entire region a few times, Jesus wraps up ministry year one in Cana of Galilee, a small town just a few miles from home.

Unfortunately, Matthew, Mark and Luke don't tell us much about what Jesus did or said during his first 12 months of ministry. John, however, adds more detail. Yet because of a general lack of information, some Bible scholars will label this first phase of Jesus' ministry his *year of obscurity.*

Navigating Jesus' Ministry

3. Ministry in Galilee

Elapsed Time   18 months (AD 27-28)
Places   Galilee

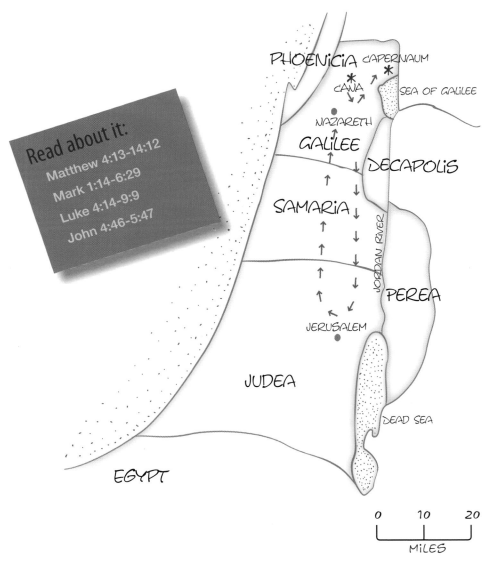

Read about it:
Matthew 4:13-14:12
Mark 1:14-6:29
Luke 4:14-9:9
John 4:46-5:47

PHOENICIA   CAPERNAUM
CANA   SEA OF GALILEE
NAZARETH
GALILEE   DECAPOLIS
SAMARIA   JORDAN RIVER
PEREA
JERUSALEM
JUDEA
DEAD SEA
EGYPT

0   10   20
MILES

Highlights

Ministry in Galilee

Jesus kicks off his second ministry phase by returning to his hometown, Nazareth, where residents are gathering for Bible study at the local synagogue on the Sabbath day. He promptly enters the building and takes a seat.

When time comes for an oral reading from the Old Testament Prophets, Jesus volunteers. A synagogue helper hands him the book of Isaiah, which he opens and begins to read.

"The Spirit of the Lord is upon ME," he reads, "because he has anointed ME to preach the gospel to the poor; he has sent ME to heal the brokenhearted, to proclaim liberty to the captives and recovery of sight to the blind, to set at liberty those who are oppressed; to proclaim the acceptable year of the Lord."

All eyes now riveted on him, Jesus closes the book, hands it back to the attendant and sits down. "Today this Scripture has been fulfilled in your hearing," he adds, making it clear to all present that Isaiah's ME is HE. Rather than giving God's Messiah a hero's welcome, the Jewish townies are highly skeptical: "Is this not Joseph's son?" they wonder. And when Jesus mentions that God's blessings often extend to non-Jewish people, they become infuriated, physically drag him out of town and try to toss him off a cliff.

Undaunted, Jesus escapes, dusts himself off and hikes 20 miles downhill to Capernaum, a fishing village on the Sea of Galilee, where he sets up his ministry headquarters. For the next 18 months, he will remain in Galilee, teaching the people about the kingdom of God and caring for their needs. Here in Galilee, Jesus delivers his famous "Sermon on the Mount."

On one occasion, Jesus travels to Jerusalem to celebrate the feast of Passover. During the visit, he stirs up a religious hornets' nest by intentionally marching his disciples through grain fields on one Sabbath day and by healing a crippled man on another. For Jewish people, both activities are strictly taboo.

Navigating Jesus' Ministry

4. Training The Twelve

Elapsed Time   6 months (AD 29)
Places   Galilee and surrounds

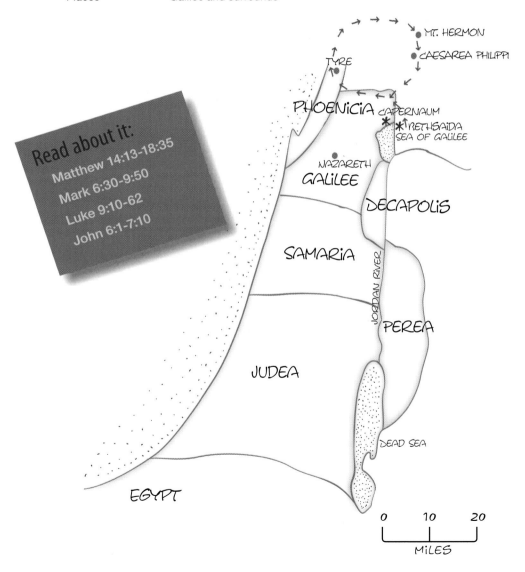

Read about it:
Matthew 14:13-18:35
Mark 6:30-9:50
Luke 9:10-62
John 6:1-7:10

MT. HERMON
CAESAREA PHILIPPI
TYRE
PHOENICIA
CAPERNAUM
BETHSAIDA
SEA OF GALILEE
NAZARETH
GALILEE
DECAPOLIS
SAMARIA
JORDAN RIVER
PEREA
JUDEA
DEAD SEA
EGYPT

0   10   20
MILES

Highlights

Training The Twelve

Realizing that his time on earth is short, Jesus selects twelve apostles to carry on his ministry and kicks off an intensive on-the-job training program for them. This personalized course in discipleship consists of a series of retreats to different locations around the region.

The trainees' first stop is on a hillside outside Bethsaida, a town on the eastern shore of the Sea of Galilee. There, Jesus teaches the team lessons of faith and dependence on God by miraculously feeding nearly ten thousand people with only five barley loaves and two fishes borrowed from a local boy's lunch.

On the way back to Capernaum, Jesus demonstrates faith to Peter by walking on water before leading the twelve northwest to Tyre and the surrounding districts.

After taking the team on a hike around Mt. Hermon, Jesus arrives at Caesarea Philippi where he stops abruptly and surprises his learners with a pop quiz.

"Who am I?", he asks them quite unexpectedly. Eleven of the twelve scrunch up their foreheads and frown. They don't have the slightest clue. Fortunately for the group, Peter ventures a guess.

"Why Jesus," he says. "You are the Christ, the Son of the living God." The training is working (…well, sort of).

Jesus wraps up this third ministry phase on a high note by taking his three senior players (Peter, James and John) on an evening prayer hike up a high mountain. As they reach the summit, Jesus gives them a sneak preview of the coming kingdom of God when before their eyes he is transfigured—his face and body dazzling with blinding, radiating light.

A few days later, the group packs up and leaves Galilee.

Navigating Jesus' Ministry

5. Road Trip

Elapsed Time   6 months (AD 29-30)
Places   Judea, Perea, Samaria,
Galilee and the Decapolis

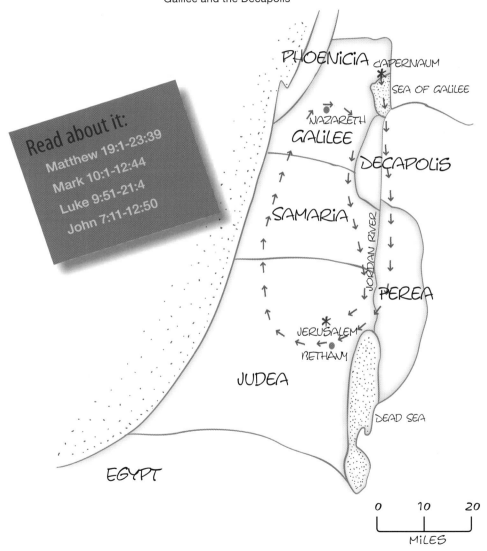

Read about it:
Matthew 19:1-23:39
Mark 10:1-12:44
Luke 9:51-21:4
John 7:11-12:50

PHOENICIA
CAPERNAUM
SEA OF GALILEE
NAZARETH
GALILEE
DECAPOLIS
SAMARIA
JORDAN RIVER
PEREA
JERUSALEM
BETHANY
JUDEA
DEAD SEA
EGYPT

0   10   20
MILES

Highlights

Road Trip

In this phase, Jesus concludes his public ministry with a six-month-long road trip from Galilee to Judea. In the Fall of AD 29, the discipleship team leaves Capernaum and slowly circles its way through each of Palestine's provinces, arriving in Jerusalem in March AD 30, just in time for the Passover feast. This journey of some 80 miles would normally take the average walker three to four days max.

But Jesus is not in a hurry; this is his farewell tour. During this trip, his teaching reaches a crescendo as he delivers his grandest parables, including the stories of the Good Samaritan and the Prodigal Son. But, as Jesus' popularity soars, violent opposition to him also builds, as the Jewish religious leaders feel threatened, and their jealous hatred reaches the boiling point.

Along the way, Jesus and his traveling team attract quite a following, their numbers swelling with every stopover. As this entourage approaches the outskirts of Jerusalem, Jesus stops in nearby Bethany at the home of Mary, Martha and Lazarus to visit his close friends one last time. That evening, the three honor Jesus and his team by hosting a wonderful dinner party.

Early the next day, which happens to be a Sunday, Jesus saddles up a young donkey and rides into Jerusalem amidst massive crowds who frantically wave palm branches and shout, "Hosanna, Hosanna," at the top of their lungs. This Hebrew word, which we have come to know as a word of praise, actually translates into, "Please save us, NOW!" It is a desperate cry for help.

On Monday morning, Jesus returns to Jerusalem and heads to the temple, his Father's house, to teach. Once inside, he cleans up the place, driving out the money changers and overturning their tables.

The next day, following a productive morning of teaching in the temple, Jesus has one final showdown with his archrivals, the Jewish religious leaders, during which he verbally roasts them for their blindness, stubbornness and indifference towards God. He then marches out of the temple grounds, never to return.

Navigating Jesus' Ministry

6. Passion Week

Elapsed Time   1 week (Spring AD 30)
Place   Jerusalem

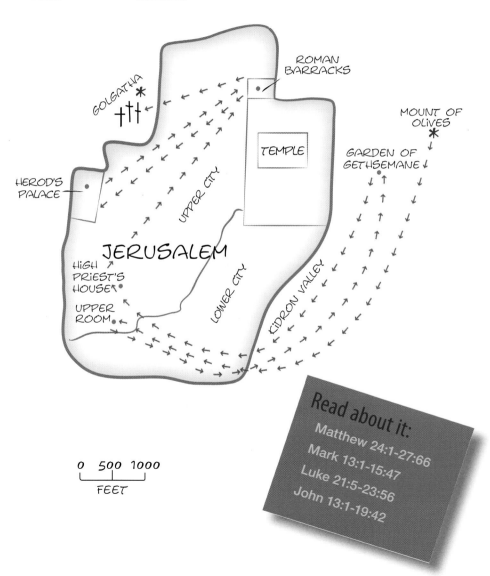

ROMAN BARRACKS

GOLGATHA

MOUNT OF OLIVES

TEMPLE

GARDEN OF GETHSEMANE

HEROD'S PALACE

UPPER CITY

JERUSALEM

HIGH PRIEST'S HOUSE

LOWER CITY

KIDRON VALLEY

UPPER ROOM

0 500 1000
FEET

Read about it:
Matthew 24:1-27:66
Mark 13:1-15:47
Luke 21:5-23:56
John 13:1-19:42

Highlights

Passion Week

On Tuesday afternoon, during this last week of his life, Jesus holds a final training session for his apostles on a green hillside of the Mount of Olives. There, the 12 pepper their Master with questions about when and how the world will end and when and how he plans to participate in its ending. Jesus answers most of their questions, mostly by parables.

Wednesday is apparently a day of rest, for the Bible is strangely silent regarding the group's activities on that day. But, by Thursday, the team is back at it, as Jesus sends Peter and John scurrying around Jerusalem to "prepare the Passover for us, so we can eat it together."

As the sun sets slowly in the west, and Passover officially begins, Jesus gathers his guys together in an upper room and opens the evening's scheduled events with a speech.

"You have no idea how much I have looked forward to eating this Passover meal with you," says Jesus fondly. "I will not eat it again until it is celebrated in God's kingdom."

During dinner, Jesus surprises the disciples by pouring water into a basin, laying aside his outer garments and washing their feet. He then dismisses Judas Iscariot, the traitor, knowing that within hours he will betray him to the authorities. As Judas slinks off into the darkness to do his dirty work (good riddance), Jesus inaugurates his *Last Supper* by sharing bread and wine with the remaining 11 apostles and spends his remaining free time in conversations with them.

Towards midnight, after Jesus says his last goodbyes, he leads the team out of the upper room and heads to a garden called Gethsemane in a river valley below Jerusalem. There, Jesus' *passion* begins.

During the next 18 hours, Jesus prays, is betrayed, is arrested, jailed, tried, convicted, beaten and humiliated. Crucified, he dies, and is buried—all to fulfill God's perfect plan of salvation.

Navigating Jesus' Ministry

7. Resurrection

Elapsed Time 40 days (Spring AD 30)
Places Jerusalem, and a few other places

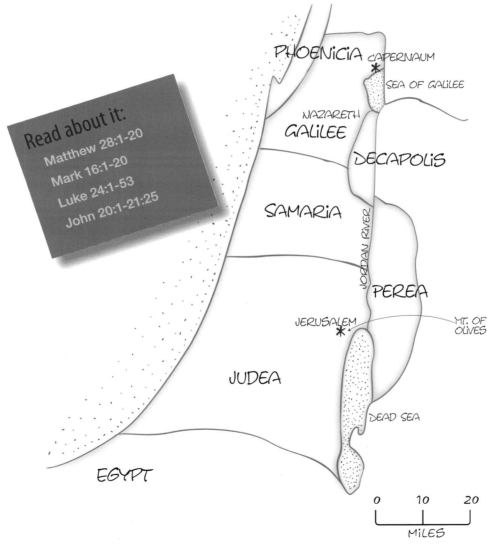

Read about it:
Matthew 28:1-20
Mark 16:1-20
Luke 24:1-53
John 20:1-21:25

PHOENICIA CAPERNAUM
SEA OF GALILEE
NAZARETH
GALILEE
DECAPOLIS
SAMARIA
JORDAN RIVER
PEREA
JERUSALEM MT. OF OLIVES
JUDEA
DEAD SEA
EGYPT

0   10   20
MILES

Highlights

Resurrection

Jesus is dead. His disciples have turned tail and are running for their lives. Peter is in deep shock, having denied Jesus publically three times and having just watched him being tortured and killed.

Things are looking pretty bleak.

But the women are there, Mary Magdalene, mother Mary and Salome, maintaining their constant vigil at Jesus' tomb. Friday night. Saturday. Saturday night.

Then early on Sunday morning, just before dawn, the earth quakes as an angel rolls a gigantic boulder away from the opening of Jesus' tomb. At first light, the women peek inside but see nothing.

Jesus is not there. He is risen! Jesus is alive!

Before long, Jesus appears to Mary Magdalene to tell her the good news. He then shows himself alive to the other women and also to Peter and two discouraged disciples who are heading out of town before making a surprise appearance at a gathering of the apostles (minus Thomas) that evening.

Over the next 40 days, Jesus remains on earth, appearing and disappearing at will and teaching his followers a few final things about the kingdom of God. During this time, over 500 people, including his half-brothers James and Jude, become eyewitnesses of his resurrection.

When the time comes that he must leave, Jesus hands off his kingdom work to his apostles and ends his earthly pilgrimage at the Mount of Olives.

There, he says one last goodbye and ascends towards heaven. The disciples gaze upwards until Jesus disappears into the clouds.

The New Testament World

ITALY

• ROME

GREECE

BLACK SEA

ASIA MINOR
(TURKEY)

• ATHENS

• EPHESUS

• NAZARETH

MEDITERRANEAN SEA

PALESTINE
(ISRAEL)

• JERUSALEM

EGYPT

ARABIA

Did you know?
Mediterranean means in the middle of the earth.

```
0       100     200
|_____|_____|
      MILES
```

The New Testament World

After our journey with Jesus through Palestine, we now expand our boundaries to the north and west to include the entire world of the New Testament. This region, about the size of the United States, has the Mediterranean Sea at its center and landmasses on its sides. To the north are Italy, Greece and Asia Minor (today's Turkey). To the south are Egypt and Arabia. All of the major activities of the New Testament happened in this region.

Roman military rule

At the time of Christ, three cultures impacted the lives of the people of this region. The first was Roman. This iron-fisted world empire ruled Palestine, where Jesus and his followers lived. And if there was an upside to ruthless military forces occupying your country, it was that the Romans also occupied all of the neighboring countries. So, peace reigned for decades. And, since the Romans were fabulous road builders, travel was easy (…well, sort of).

Greek culture

For centuries before Christ, the Greeks were famous for their love of education, philosophy, architecture and the arts. During the reign of Alexander the Great, the Greeks dominated the world and established their culture in hundreds of cities they built. Two of these cities, Sepphoris and Scythopolis were located in Palestine, not far from Nazareth, where Jesus grew up.

Jewish religion

The practice of Jewish religion, with its belief in the Bible's one true God, also impacted life in the region during these times. Prior to Jesus' birth, religious persecutions that broke out in Palestine had scattered devout Jews across the known world. As a result, more Jewish people lived outside the Holy Land than inside it. As the Hebrews built synagogues in every major city, Jewish religion and the knowledge of God spread throughout the region.

The Origin of the New Testament

Inspired

The Bible is a collection of 66 sacred writings (39 in the Old Testament, 27 in the New Testament), created by faithful men who were moved by God's Spirit to pick up their pens. The belief that these "books" were divinely inspired is the primary and determining factor that makes them special and unique.

Written

Most Bible scholars believe that all of the 27 books of the New Testament were written during a 50-year period, from approximately AD 50-100. Though dates are not explicitly mentioned by any of the writers, historical events, names of political figures and other information included in their books have helped researchers determine approximate publication dates.

Circulated

After the books of the New Testament were written, they were copied, circulated and used extensively by Christian communities for the spiritual benefit of the members, a practice that continued for nearly 300 years.

Confirmed

In the late fourth century, church leaders became concerned about the proliferation of religious fiction and forged writings that were finding their way into the churches. As a result, church councils were convened to confirm the inspired works and to weed out the fakes.

In North Africa, at the third Council of Carthage (AD 397), the Bible's 66 books were officially deemed *divinely inspired*, including the 27 books that make up our New Testament today.

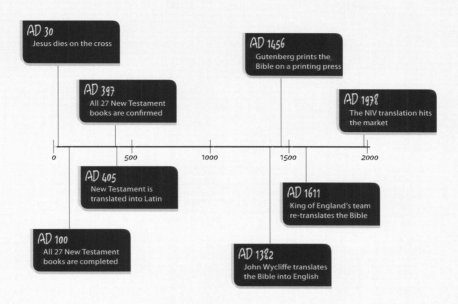

Did you know…

- There were no chapter numbers in the New Testament until 1205 when Stephen Langton, Archbishop of Canterbury, devised a numbering system.

- There were no verse numbers in the New Testament until 1551 when a book publisher, Robert Stephanus, divided the chapters into verses (by himself).

- The King James Version (1611) is still available for sale 400 years after its first printing. Over the years, billions of copies have been printed.

Book Groups—the Mother of all Frameworks

The 27 books of the New Testament are organized in six groups, symbolized by **frameworks'** logo, the six boxes on the opposite page.

Biographies

The first four books are biographies of the life of Jesus Christ. Each takes a distinct point of view, yet all harmonize with one another. The name of each book is the name of its writer.

History

The second group is a group of one: the book of Acts, which is modern day shorthand for *The Acts of the Apostles*. Acts is a history book that records the activities surrounding the development of the Christian church during the 40-year period after Christ's ascension to heaven.

Paul's letters to churches

The third group is a cluster of nine separate letters (they're not really books) written by the Apostle Paul to Christian churches in different locations. The name of each letter usually comes from the name of the city where the recipients lived. Romans, for example, was written to Christians living in Rome (and so on).

Paul's letters to people

The fourth group is a handful of personal letters, written by Paul to three of his co-workers. The name of each letter is the name of the recipient.

General letters

The fifth group is a collection of eight letters from five writers destined for circulation among general audiences. The name of each letter is the name of the writer, except Hebrews, which means, Jewish people.

Prophecy

The last group is also a group of one: Revelation, a book that reveals a unique picture of Jesus and speaks of present and future world events.

| 4 | 1 | 9 | 4 | 8 | 1 |

Biographies of Christ	History	Paul's Letters to Churches	Paul's Letters to People	General Letters	Prophecy
Matthew	Acts	Romans	1 Timothy	Hebrews	Revelation
Mark		1 Corinthians	2 Timothy	James	
Luke		2 Corinthians	Titus	1 Peter	
John		Galatians	Philemon	2 Peter	
		Ephesians		1 John	
		Phillipians		2 John	
		Colossians		3 John	
		1 Thessalonians		Jude	
		2 Thessalonians			

Writers

Eight men wrote the books (and letters) of the New Testament. Here they are, presented in the order in which their books (and letters) appear.

Matthew

Also called Levi. One of Jesus' original 12 apostles (trainees). A Jewish businessman and resident of Capernaum in Galilee who was good with numbers and words. Worked for the Roman government collecting taxes (customs duties), and because of this, was bitterly despised by his fellow Jews, who hated the Romans. Jesus asked him point blank to "follow me." Matthew did and soon became fiercely loyal to his new Master.

Mark

Formally, John Mark. John was his Jewish name, and Mark was his Roman name. NOT one of the original 12 apostles. Lived in Jerusalem. As a young man would have seen Jesus and heard him speak. His mother Mary, a widow, is one of six Marys you'll meet in the New Testament (I know, it's confusing). She hosted prayer meetings for church leaders at their home in Jerusalem. Before completing his Gospel, Mark apprenticed under both Peter and Paul.

Luke

A Greek medical doctor, possibly from the city of Antioch in Syria. Also a seafarer, historian and evangelist who wrote two New Testament books—Luke and Acts. Close friend and traveling companion of Paul. Became a pastor of the church in Philippi for a time. Accompanied Paul to Rome for his trial before Caesar and remained there with him. May have been a blood brother of Titus, another of Paul's co-workers. Probably did not meet Jesus.

John

Jesus' cousin and one of his original 12 apostles. John's mom, Salome, and Mary, Jesus' mom, were sisters. A fisherman by trade. He and his older brother James (also one of the 12) worked in their father Zebedee's fishing business in Galilee. John was the disciple "whom Jesus loved." He stood by Jesus at the cross and took care of Mary after Jesus' death. The longest living original apostle. Wrote two New Testament books, John and Revelation, and three letters.

Paul

Saul, his Jewish name; Paul, his Roman name. Well-educated son of a Jewish religious leader and an exceptional student. A tent-maker by profession. A Bible expert who was also well-versed in Greek literature. At age 35, he was a fanatical Jewish legalist who hated Christians until Jesus himself paid him a visit, knocked him down and then recruited him. Became the greatest Christian missionary and Bible teacher of all time. Given credit for writing 13 New Testament letters—and possibly wrote a 14th (Hebrews).

James

One of four men named James in your New Testament. Half-brother of Jesus, yet did not believe in Jesus' divinity while growing up with him. Came to faith as an eyewitness of Christ's resurrection and received the Spirit's baptism at Pentecost. Rose to a leadership position in the early church in Jerusalem. Known for strongly supporting Jewish law, almost to a fault, and the Jews' need for salvation in Christ. Wrote one New Testament letter.

Peter

Jewish fisherman from Galilee whom Jesus called to be a *fisher of men*. Has three Bible names: Simon (natural name), Peter (which means "rock" in Greek) and Cephas (Peter, in the Aramaic language). One of the original 12 and the most colorful of all New Testament characters. His brother, Andrew, introduced him to Jesus. Partner of John in their fishing business. Denied affiliation with Jesus three times. Then became the greatest evangelist and apostle to the Jewish people. Led thousands to faith. Wrote two New Testament letters.

Jude

Little-known half-brother of Jesus who, like his brother, James, did not *believe in Jesus* until after Christ's resurrection. Preacher. Evangelist. Defender of the faith. Had a heart for Jewish Christians. His is the last in a string of 21 New Testament letters.

Translations

Did you know...

Our English New Testament was translated from Greek

Greek was the common language of the first century, much like English is in today's world. Over the years, Bible translators followed one of three approaches in translating the New Testament from Greek into English:

Word-for-word—a literal approach that tries to translate each Greek word into the same English word. The object is accuracy.

Thought-for-thought—a phrase-by-phrase approach that conveys the meaning of each Greek phrase in English. The object is readability.

Balanced—a blend of the two approaches, translating word-for-word when it's readable and thought-for-thought when it isn't.

Everyone should buy two Bibles

One for study and one for reading. Buy yourself a good word-for-word study version to give you the accuracy you need to dig into the details. And for your reading enjoyment, buy yourself a thought-for-thought reading version. Here are the most popular translations (and their abbreviations). If you own one from each group, you can't go wrong:

Study versions
- New King James Version (NKJV)
- New International Version (NIV)
- English Standard Version (ESV)

Reading versions
- New Living Translation (NLT)
- The Message (TM)—a paraphrase

Dates of Writings

Book	Writer	Approx Date	Book	Writer	Approx Date
Biographies			**Paul's letters to people**		
Matthew	Matthew	AD 64	1 Timothy	Paul	AD 65
Mark	Mark	AD 63	2 Timothy	Paul	AD 67
Luke	Luke	AD 64	Titus	Paul	AD 66
John	John	AD 80	Philemon	Paul	AD 63
History			**General letters**		
Acts	Luke	AD 65	Hebrews	Paul ?	AD 66
Paul's letters to churches			James	James	AD 50
Romans	Paul	AD 59	1 Peter	Peter	AD 64
1 Corinthians	Paul	AD 57	2 Peter	Peter	AD 64
2 Corinthians	Paul	AD 58	1 John	John	AD 85
Galatians	Paul	AD 55	2 John	John	AD 85
Ephesians	Paul	AD 63	3 John	John	AD 85
Philippians	Paul	AD 63	Jude	Jude	AD 64
Colossians	Paul	AD 63	**Prophecy**		
1 Thessalonians	Paul	AD 53	Revelation	John	AD 95
2 Thessalonians	Paul	AD 53			

As you look at the dates listed in the table on the opposite page, notice that the writings were not placed in chronological order. Also be aware that there are legitimate differences of opinion regarding the dates of the books and letters of the New Testament. The timeline below includes generally accepted dates (small numbers below) and shows how the writings clustered together.

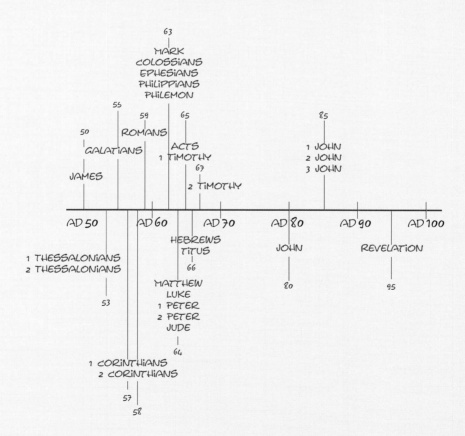

Length and Order

If you were to lay the New Testament books and letters side by side (opposite page) to compare their length, a number of things might pop off the page at you. First, you might notice that some of the books (Luke, Matthew, Acts) are quite long and that some of the letters (2 John, 3 John) are very brief. You might also discover that, lo and behold, in some cases, there appears to be a relationship between the order of the books and page count.

Biographies

Luke's Gospel is the longest of the four biographies of Christ. Mark's book is by far the shortest, just over half as long as Luke's.

History

Acts, Luke's second volume, is only slightly shorter than his Gospel. Together, they make Luke the second most-prolific writer of the New Testament, following Paul.

Paul's letters to churches

Take a look at this group as a whole. Can you see that these letters are placed in order of descending length? Romans is placed first because it's the longest, and 2 Thessalonians is last because it's the shortest. Does this surprise you?

Paul's letters to people

Here we go again. 1 Timothy is placed first because it is longest, and Philemon is last because it is shortest. Who would have thought?

General letters

Hebrews, the longest general letter, is placed first in this cluster, while Jude is last. John's three little letters are grouped together.

Prophecy

John closes the New Testament, and the entire Bible for that matter, with his book of Revelation, his fifth contribution to the Scriptures. It has been said, and rightfully so, that John always has the last word.

Biographies		Number of Pages (one square represents one page)
Matthew	41 ½	□□□ ½
Mark	26 ½	□□□□□□□□□□□□□□□□□□□□□□□□□□ ½
Luke	44 ½	□□ ½
John	33	□□□□□□□□□□□□□□□□□□□□□□□□□□□□□□□□□□□

History

Acts	41	□□□

Paul's letters to churches

Romans	17	□□□□□□□□□□□□□□□□□
1 Corinthians	15	□□□□□□□□□□□□□□□
2 Corinthians	11	□□□□□□□□□□□
Galatians	6	□□□□□□
Ephesians	5 ½	□□□□□ ½
Philippians	4	□□□□
Colossians	3 ½	□□□ ½
1 Thessalonians	3	□□□
2 Thessalonians	2	□□

Paul's letters to people

1 Timothy	4	□□□□
2 Timothy	3	□□□
Titus	2	□□
Philemon	1	□

General letters

Hebrews	13	□□□□□□□□□□□□□
James	4 ½	□□□□ ½
1 Peter	4 ½	□□□□ ½
2 Peter	3	□□□
1 John	4 ½	□□□□ ½
2 John	½	½
3 John	½	½
Jude	1 ½	□ ½

Prophecy

Revelation	20 ½	□□□□□□□□□□□□□□□□□□□□ ½

Book Frameworks and Themes
Part 2

Book Chapter Format

With Part One, the Framework of the New Testament as a foundation, we come to Part Two, the individual books. Before proceeding, we'll stop to look briefly at the first four books—Matthew, Mark, Luke and John—as a group.

Your journey will then continue with guided tours of each book, one at a time. The agenda for each book is the list of 10 questions that was presented in the introduction. Here they are again:

1. **Intro—What is this book like?**

    A full-page color photograph and a short story create compelling mental images that describe what the book is like. These pages make the book easier for you to understand.

2. **Theme—What is this book about?**

    A sticky tagline, crisp imagery and a short narrative help you visualize the book's theme. Try to memorize all 27 themes and the books they describe. To remember them is to know the main topic of each book.

3. **Purpose—Why was it written?**

    Knowing the circumstances that surround the writing of a book helps you understand its content and purpose. Here you'll read a story about the book's origin. Since historical details are often sketchy, scholars' views sometimes differ regarding the book's primary purpose. For the smaller books, this section is combined with the Intro or Theme.

4. **Outline—How is the book organized?**

    A brief outline, presented both in text and graphical formats, gives you a map of the book's structure and parts. The illustrations (stacks of pages) show you the sections of each book that are longer (or shorter).

5. **Verses—How does it read?**

   One dozen Bible verses, selected from the book, substantiate its theme and introduce you to the writer's style. Each quotation is labeled with a chapter and verse notation to help you locate it in the Bible. For example, Matt 6:10 means: the book of Matthew, chapter 6, verse 10.

6. **Navigation—How do I move through it?**

   This section contains helpful hints to keep in mind as you begin to read the book on your own. These instructions make suggestions of what to look for as you read. They highlight the best places to invest your time.

7. **Unique things—What makes this book or its author special?**

   Here are a few fascinating, little known facts that make each book enjoyable, unique and memorable. They also make great conversation starters to surprise your friends over coffee: Say, did you know…?

8. **Recap—What should I remember most?**

   Questions 1-7 have built conceptual **frameworks** for the book. Now it's time to read the book. But before you do, here are a few key points to remember. The **Read it**! section gives you estimated reading times.

9. **Questions—How can I explore further or go deeper?**

   A few thought-provoking questions will stimulate group discussions and help your personal study. These are also great jumping off points for deeper exploration.

10. **Insights—What one verse can I apply right now?**

    Each chapter ends with a brief commentary on one verse from the book. Like icing on a cake, this page gives you an opportunity to enrich your study by applying one of the book's thoughts to your life.

Biographies of Christ

The Four Gospels

In two groups

Because the four Gospels show different sides of Jesus' life and work, they can be thought of in two separate groups. Matthew, Mark and Luke form one group and John forms the other. Knowing this helps set the context for your reading. Here are a few ways the two groups differ:

Matthew, Mark and Luke

- Show Jesus' human side
- Show Jesus' outward activities
- Show Jesus' public events
- Are roughly chronological

John

- Shows Jesus' divine side
- Shows Jesus' inward being
- Shows Jesus' private conversations
- Ranges freely in time and place

In four different regions

places. Matthew wrote to the Jews in Palestine, Mark wrote to the Romans in Italy, Luke wrote to the Greeks in Greece and John wrote to the people living in Asia Minor. By God's sovereign design, among them, they reached the entire New Testament world (nice).

Pictured by Four Living Creatures

John receives the visions contained in his book of Revelation while he is in exile on the island of Patmos, a small rock of a place 24 miles out in the Aegean Sea, just off the coast of Turkey. The Romans had sent him there as punishment for his insistence on preaching the Word of God and evangelizing people.

One day, while John is minding his own business, Jesus suddenly appears to him from out of nowhere, scaring him half to death. After John regains his composure, Jesus invites him to come to heaven to see something spectacular.

Before he knows what hit him, John, spiritually or physically, is transported heavenward. When he arrives at his destination, he is blinded by the brilliant light of God's glorious presence radiating in all directions from a centrally-located throne.

Surrounding God's throne are four curious-looking angelic beings that are praising and worshipping God. They remind John of *living creatures* back home on planet earth. The first looks like a **lion**, the second like an **ox**. The third has the face of a **man**, and the fourth looks like a flying **eagle** (Revelation 4:6-7).

What could these creatures be, wonders John, a question that has intrigued Bible teachers for years. Some think that, since these beings are full of eyes, they symbolize God's infinite wisdom. Others suggest that they might represent earth's six groups of creatures (minus creeping things and fish), honoring their Creator.

But the best explanation might be that these beings present four dominant characteristics of Jesus Christ himself, as pictured in the four Gospels. Just as each creature has its own unique qualities and strengths, each Gospel emphasizes a different aspect of Jesus' life and ministry. Together they give us a comprehensive picture of our Savior.

What makes this explanation even more fascinating is that Revelation presents the **lion, ox, man** and **eagle** in the exact order as they appear in the Gospels—Matthew, Mark, Luke and John.

Creature	Feature	Jesus As	Gospel
Lion	Ruling authority	The King	Matthew
Ox	Tireless activity	God's Servant	Mark
Man	Human compassion	The Man	Luke
Eagle	Divine power	God	John

Intro to Matthew

It's no accident that Matthew's Gospel, regarded by some as "the most important book in the world," is the first piece of writing you will encounter as you begin your spiritual journey through the pages of the New Testament.

At once outrageously popular, Matthew's biography of the life of Christ quickly achieved bestseller status, so to speak, because it featured the most complete teachings of Jesus. For decades after it was written, Christians everywhere, who were seeking to pattern their lives by the teachings of their Master, found this book both incredibly useful and irresistibly compelling.

You will, too.

As you wander through the pages of this beautiful, well-constructed biography, be sure to notice Jesus' great speeches—there will be five of them—that will suddenly rise up like **skyscrapers** and dominate the skyline in front of you.

In each speech, Jesus tackles a different question about the Kingdom of Heaven, that mysterious, spiritual realm he came to earth to establish. As a group, these five talks dominate two-thirds of the acreage of the entire book.

Weaving their way around and between these massive structures, like quaint, well-lit city streets, are the many fascinating stories of Jesus' life and ministry, selected specifically by Matthew to support the royal theme of his book. These are the true tales of wise men traveling from afar to honor Jesus' birth. Of lepers being cleansed. Of water being walked on. Of Hosannas being shouted. Of the dead being raised.

And as you stroll along Matthew's avenues, stay alert. For there's an excellent chance that as you turn that next corner, you'll run smack dab into the monarch of the kingdom himself, God's lion, Jesus.

Matthew's theme:
God's lion roars

Matthew

Writer   Matthew
Date Written   AD 64
Place Written   Antioch, Syria
Recipients   Jews and Jewish Christians
Theme   God's lion roars

"I have been given all authority in heaven and on earth."

—Matthew 28:18

Four powerful images give rise to the themes of Matthew, Mark, Luke and John. As mentioned earlier, these are the four living creatures which surround the throne of God in the opening chapters of the book of Revelation. The first is like a lion, the second, like an ox. The third has the face of a man, and the fourth looks like a flying eagle. The lion has characteristics that correspond with the attributes of Jesus in Matthew, the first Gospel.

Lions, the dominant and most heralded members of the *big cat* family (lions, tigers, leopards and jaguars), have roamed the planet, without natural enemies, since pre-historic times. Their size, strength, quickness and majestic manes have earned them both the respect of all the other animals and the title, *King of the beasts*.

Lions are mentioned frequently in Proverbs, an Old Testament book that highlights a number of their more prominent features. Strength and courage, for example. Proverbs 30:30 says, "the lion, king of animals… won't turn aside for anything." And majesty. In Proverbs 30:29, lions are said to walk as if they were kings and move as kings do. Lions just *look* regal.

Matthew's Jesus is a roaring lion: a King who is mighty in works, reigning in life and courageous in the face of death. But more than anything else, it is Jesus' speeches that make Matthew's Christ unique. He has a lot of important things to say. And as Amos prophesied in the Old Testament, "The lion has roared—so who isn't frightened? The Sovereign Lord has spoken…" (Amos 3:8).

Why this book was written

Matthew, a despised Jewish tax collector and a social misfit, was hand-picked by Jesus, Lord knows why, to be one of the twelve Apostles who would carry on his ministry after he was gone.

One day at work, while Matthew was minding his own business, performing his usual customs officer duties of collecting tolls and extorting money from cross-country shippers, Jesus stopped by for a chat.

"Follow me," Jesus said.

To everyone's utter shock and amazement, Matthew did just that, leaving behind both a lucrative career and a luxurious lifestyle to join Jesus' traveling team. The Master's call had somehow radically changed his life.

Before heading out on the road with the team, Matthew threw a blowout farewell party for his outcast friends and invited Jesus as the guest of honor. The place was packed to the rafters. He wanted all of his guests to meet Jesus—and that afternoon, many did.

Three years later, shortly after Jesus had returned to heaven, God called Matthew to begin his own ministry by spreading the good news of salvation to his Jewish countrymen in Palestine and in the surrounding regions.

To reach a wider audience, God inspired him to write a biography of Jesus' life from a Jewish person's point of view. His objective was to convince his readers that Jesus, whom the Jews had rejected, was indeed the Messiah they had been expecting. For this reason, Matthew referenced the Old Testament over 90 times as he composed his biography.

And to demonstrate that Jesus was a direct descendent of David, Israel's greatest king, and of Abraham, the father of the Jewish nation, he boldly displayed Christ's family tree on the very first page of his book, as if he was saying, "Any questions?"

A brief outline of the book

In this simple outline of Matthew's book, Jesus' five major speeches rise heavenward out of the surrounding landscape. Take a good look at the piles of pages below. Or study the outline. Either way, you can't miss them.

From beginning to end, Matthew's central point is abundantly clear—God's lion is roaring—so open up your ears and listen.

	Chapters
Jesus the King is born, introduced and starts speaking	1-4
1st Speech—How my kingdom operates	5-7
2nd Speech—How my disciples work	10
3rd Speech—What my kingdom is like	13
4th Speech—How to thrive in my kingdom	18
5th Speech—When my kingdom will come	24-25
Jesus is crucified, conquers death and reigns	27-28

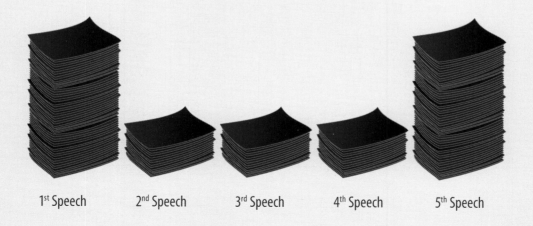

1st Speech   2nd Speech   3rd Speech   4th Speech   5th Speech

Verses that present Jesus as the King

As you read the following words spoken by Jesus, notice how he uses the terms *king* and *kingdom* repeatedly in his speeches. By showcasing these particular sayings of Jesus, Matthew is being intentional about driving home *one* point—Jesus is the King.

"Where is the newborn king of the Jews?" **Matthew 2:2**

"Repent of your sins and turn to God, for the Kingdom of Heaven is near." **3:2**

"May your Kingdom come soon. May your will be done on earth, as it is in heaven." **6:10**

"Seek the Kingdom of God above all else...and he will give you everything you need." **6:33**

"Not everyone who calls out to me, 'Lord! Lord!' will enter the Kingdom of Heaven." **7:21**

"The Kingdom of Heaven is like a farmer who planted good seed in his field." **13:24**

"The Kingdom of Heaven is like a mustard seed planted in a field." **13:31**

"The Kingdom of Heaven is like the yeast a woman used in making bread." **13:33**

"The Kingdom of Heaven is like a treasure that a man discovered hidden in a field." **13:44**

"Again, the Kingdom of Heaven is like a merchant on the lookout for choice pearls." **13:45**

"The Kingdom of Heaven can be illustrated by the story of ten bridesmaids..." **25:1**

"Come, you who are blessed by my Father, inherit the Kingdom prepared for you..." **25:34**

How to navigate Matthew

1. **Notice that Jesus' royal ancestry is placed first**

   Turn to chapter one. Read verses 1-17. Notice how Matthew opens his book with Jesus' family tree. Read all of the names (if you can). You will end up at Jesus. Matthew has done this on purpose. All kings have pedigrees to authenticate their bloodlines and establish their right to the throne. This is Christ's.

2. **Read Jesus' five speeches**

   Set aside time to read each one of Jesus' five speeches. On your first time through, please don't try to figure out everything you read. Just try to visualize King Jesus speaking comfortably with his loyal subjects, explaining to them how things work in his kingdom. Here they are: Matthew 5:1-7:28; 10:1-42; 13:1-53; 18:1-35; 24:1-25:46

3. **Be on the lookout for Old Testament references**

   There will be 90 of them. Turn to Matthew 2:5-6. Here Matthew quotes an Old Testament prophet and says, "this is what the prophet wrote." Now look at 2:17-18 where it says, "what the Lord had spoken through the prophet." These are your telltale clues. Watch for them.

4. **Notice how the story ends**

   Turn to the last page of the book. Read Matthew 28:16-20. Here Jesus says that he has been given all authority in heaven and on earth (this means he is the king) and that he will always be with us. His kingdom is here to stay (think about it).

Unique things about Matthew

Did you know...

Matthew includes foreign dignitaries

Only Matthew mentions the "We three kings of orient are," so called, who bearing gifts had traveled afar to visit Jesus soon after his birth. These "kings" are not mentioned anywhere else in the Bible. Only here, in the book of the lion-king. Nor, by the way, does the Bible say that there were only three, or that these wise men were kings.

Tax collectors obsess on money

Matthew, a recovering tax collector, speaks more about money and coins than any other Bible writer. This book contains more terms for money—nine different words—than any other book in the Bible.

Matthew speaks of the Kingdom of Heaven

Of the four Gospel writers, only Matthew uses the phrase "Kingdom of Heaven" when referring to Christ's kingdom. This expression conveys both the location of Christ's future realm and the nature of the life we can experience today with Jesus. To drive home this two-fold theme, Matthew repeats these three words over 30 times in 28 chapters.

This book is a bridge

Matthew's book was placed first in your New Testament on purpose. Its function is to link the mission and message of Christ with the Old Testament that predicted his coming. It is the bridge that joins the two halves of your Bible together.

Recap

- When you think of the book of Matthew, think of a modern city with five prominent skyscrapers. These tall buildings symbolize Jesus' five major speeches.

- In Matthew, picture Jesus as a lion, roaring as he speaks. He has a lot to say, and he commands everyone's attention.

- As you read this book, remember that Matthew's purpose is to convince the Jewish people that Jesus is their Messiah, God's anointed Savior. This is why Matthew uses 90 references to the Old Testament in his book.

Read it!

- Read Matthew now. At a casual reading pace, total reading time is 2 hours. You can finish it in six 20-minute sessions.

Self-study / Group Discussion Questions

- What is it about the book of Matthew that might cause some to regard it as "the most important book in the world"?

- In what ways do you imagine that Jesus, God's Lion, is like other lions? In what ways might he be different?

- Matthew introduces Jesus to his readers as the King of the kingdom of the heavens. How might Jesus' kingdom be similar to other kingdoms on the earth? How might it be unique?

Insights that we can apply today

"You (believers) are the salt (preservative) of the earth."

—Matthew 5:13

Salt prevents decay and purifies. Salt makes things good. Salt seasons and brings out foods' natural flavors. Jesus says that his followers are the salt of the earth. Do you believe this about yourself? Did you know that your presence in your family, workplace, or social group can make a tangible, positive difference in people's lives and can bring out the best in them?

Intro to Mark

If Matthew's book is like five gleaming skyscrapers towering above a modern city, Mark's could be considered humble huts cobbled together in some forlorn and forgotten village. As far as popularity goes, to the earliest Gospel readers, there was simply no comparison. Matthew completely dominated the landscape. Mark was dwarfed in his shadow.

This is actually quite surprising, since at that time many people knew that Mark's book was not really Mark's book at all. It was the great Apostle Peter's book, written down in Mark's words. But we'll get to that later.

For now, picture a stubby little book that though divine-inspired, was overlooked by Christians—for 1,800 years.

But then one day in 1863, in Leipzig, Germany of all places, everything changed. A promising young Bible student by the name of Heinrich Julius Holtzmann published a book titled *Die Synoptischen Evangelelein* (The Synoptic Gospels) which would radically change Mark's destiny.

Using theories developed previously by other scholars, Holtzmann argued persuasively that Mark was the first Gospel written—not Matthew, as had long been supposed.

"The immediate response to Holtzman's work brought Mark to a place of prominence," said Walter Wessel, Professor of New Testament at Bethel Theological Seminary. "Mark was seen as the original Gospel, containing the uninterpreted historical facts about Jesus of Nazareth... Mark was considered to be pure gospel."

Within a short time, as many well-known theologians jumped on the Holtzmann bandwagon, Mark's popularity soared. Christian readers flocked to it. The second Gospel became a **rock star**—overnight.

The scholars who began to pore over Mark's pages soon discovered that they held in their hands a hidden gem. In no other Gospel had they found such detailed reporting of Jesus' activities. Or such vivid language. Or so many miracles. Mark's book had made it to the big time.

Mark's theme:
God's ox dies

Mark

Writer   Mark
Date Written   AD 63
Place Written   Italy
Recipients   Romans
Theme   God's ox dies

"For even the Son of Man came not to be served but to serve and to give his life as a ransom for many." —Mark 10:45

The ox, the second of the four living creatures pictured in Revelation, can be used to illustrate the Jesus we find in Mark's Gospel. At once extremely powerful, yet fully obedient, the temperament and qualities of this hard-working bovine are strikingly similar to Mark's Christ in two ways.

First, in Bible times, the ox was considered the most valuable animal a person could own. For this reason, Sir William Smith sang the praises of oxen in his world-famous *Smith's Bible Dictionary*, first published in London in 1863.

> "There was no animal in the rural economy of the Israelites, or indeed in that of the ancient Orientals generally, that was held in higher esteem than the ox; and deservedly so, for the ox was the animal upon whose patient labors depended all the ordinary operations of farming."

In those days oxen served their masters long and hard by plowing fields, treading out corn, pumping water, turning millstones, transporting passengers and feeding people, among other things. They could pull heavy loads great distances long after horses and donkeys would have given up.

Likewise, in the first half of Mark we see Jesus, the Son of God, pictured as God's faithful and tireless ox working day and night, to serve God by serving mankind.

Second, in the Old Testament, oxen took on another, more personal role. In the worship of God, animals were given as *sin offerings* to atone for the sins of the people. Oxen were the supreme sacrifice, offered to absolve the sins of the entire nation. This foreshadowed Christ, in the second half of Mark's book, as God's perfect sacrifice, dying for the sins of the world.

Why this book was written

Mark, or John Mark as he was more properly known, was a young follower of Christ who, in the years after Jesus' departure, had developed a close relationship with Peter. The two traveled together extensively, spreading the Good News to whoever would listen. At each stop along the way, Mark listened carefully as Peter repeated his eyewitness accounts of Jesus' life.

According to tradition, on one occasion, while they visited Rome, and after hearing Peter's messages countless times, Mark was approached by members of the church in Rome who asked him to write down Peter's preachings for their local use. Mark, with Peter's blessing, did just that.

Mark knew that Romans were people of action—and that they loved to honor mighty, purpose-driven men as their heroes. So it's no surprise that as he started writing, he was inspired to present Jesus as God's mighty, purpose-driven servant who had been sent from heaven to earth to save mankind.

By choosing action words, and by intentionally creating long run-on sentences, Mark succeeded in creating *motion pictures* for his Roman audience to watch. In scene after scene, his readers would see an ox of a man knocking down social barriers and pushing his mission forward more tenaciously than any other man on earth ever had.

In this way, Mark built momentum into his narrative through the first 15 of the book's 16 chapters. Then, *POW!* The storyline reaches a crescendo at the foot of Christ's cross, where after Jesus sacrifices his life so that all mankind might live, a Roman military commander stands up and shouts, "This man truly was the Son of God!"

A brief outline of the book

Mark's Gospel breaks neatly into two large chunks. The first 10 chapters introduce us to Jesus the Slave who works like an ox to help people everywhere.

The second six chapters show us Jesus the Hero who volunteers to die so that all people may live. God's lowly slave becomes mankind's mighty hero. This story is very impressive, especially to Roman minds.

	Chapters
Jesus serves others	
God's ox arrives and immediately goes to work	1
He works night and day in northern Palestine	2-6
He pushes his work relentlessly into other regions	7-10
Jesus sacrifices himself	
He sacrifices his life to save mankind	11-15
The Roman centurion calls him the *"Son of God"*	15
Jesus, mankind's mighty hero, conquers death	16

Jesus serves others   Jesus sacrifices himself

Verses that capture images of God's ox on the move

Read the following verses without stopping to take a breath.

Jesus called out to them… and they left their nets **at once**. **Mark 1:17-18**

The news about Jesus spread **quickly** *throughout the entire region.* **1:28**

Instantly *the leprosy disappeared, and the man was healed.* **1:42**

When Jesus returned… the news spread **quickly** *that he was back home.* **2:1**

Jesus knew **immediately** *what they were thinking.* **2:8**

And the girl… **immediately** *stood up and walked around!* **5:42**

Immediately *after this, Jesus insisted that his disciples get back into the boat.* **6:45**

The people recognized Jesus **at once**. **6:54**

Right away *a woman who had heard about him came.* **7:25**

Instantly *the man could hear perfectly.* **7:35**

Immediately *after this, he got into a boat.* **8:10**

The father **instantly** *cried out, "I do believe…"* **9:24**

If you feel out of breath, congratulations. Mark has succeeded in bringing you into his fast moving narrative.

How to navigate Mark

1. **Notice that Mark opens his book with action**

    Read Mark 1:1. Right off the bat, Jesus is introduced as the Son of God. No ifs, ands or buts. Eight short verses later, Jesus is baptized, and *immediately* is off and running. There he goes. Catch him if you can.

2. **Experience Mark's run-ons first-hand**

    Find yourself a King James Version of the Bible. Get pencil and paper. Open to Mark chapter three. As you read the chapter word by word, make a *mark* (awesome) on your paper every time Mark uses the word ***and***. Now count the number of ***ands***. How many do you have? Does this surprise you? (The answer can be found in Notes in the back of this book.)

3. **Be on the lookout for eyewitness details**

    Mark 4:38 says that Jesus had "his head on a cushion." Mark 3:5 says that Jesus "looked around at them angrily." Only an eyewitness could know these and other vivid details. In this case, it was Peter.

4. **Read more miracles**

    In 16 chapters, Mark records 18 of Jesus' miracles. In their books, Matthew, Luke and John include far fewer. The reason for this is simple. Mark knew that Christ's mighty deeds would impress his macho Roman readers.

Unique things about Mark

Did you know...

Mark is Mr. Run-on

Mark is the king of run-on sentences, and this is no accident because, by using the word *and* over 1,300 times and by smooshing endless sentences together without ever taking a break, he forces his readers to see Jesus as a real mover and shaker, which is exactly what he intends to do (whew).

Call me Stump-fingers

Tradition tells us that Mark's nickname was "Stump-fingers," which doesn't sound like a fun nickname to have at all. They say that his fingers were unusually short, but who knows for sure? It didn't affect his writing. Some day we can ask him.

Poor starts—great finishes

When Jesus was betrayed, Peter denied him three times. Peter later became Jesus' greatest disciple. Likewise, as a young man, Mark miserably failed Paul during an important missionary journey they took together. When the going got tough, Mark bailed out and headed home to Jerusalem. Years later, he became Paul's valued co-worker and was used by God to write one of the books of the Bible, the Gospel of Mark.

A naked teenager runs away

Tradition tells us that Mark wrote himself into the storyline of his own book. In Mark 14:51, as Jesus is being arrested in the garden of Gethsemane, a young man (presumably Mark) is hanging around watching what's going on. When the Romans try to grab him, he takes off so fast that he runs out of his clothes.

Recap

- Remember that Mark's Gospel was completely overlooked for 1,800 years. Then it became as popular as a rock star overnight.

- Visualize Jesus as God's ox—a strong, obedient, hard-working servant. In Jesus' selfless sacrifice, the Romans could see a new kind of hero.

- Mark breaks neatly into two chunks. The first 10 chapters show Jesus serving others; the last six show Jesus sacrificing his life for others.

Read it!

- Read Mark now. At a casual reading pace, total reading time is 1 hour and 20 minutes. You can finish it in four 20-minute sessions.

Self-study / Group discussion questions

- In Matthew, Jesus is like a roaring lion who has a lot to say. In Mark, he is like a powerful ox, moving constantly, but saying little. Which of these personality traits of Christ—rich speaking or effective doing—are you drawn to more? Why?

- Which is more important: what we say or what we do? Or are both equally important? Why?

- The first part of Mark tells the story of how Jesus came to serve others by meeting their deepest needs. The second part tells how Jesus went to the cross to sacrifice his life to save us from death. Is one of these two activities more critical than the other?

Insights that we can apply today

"How hard it is for the rich to enter the Kingdom of God." —Mark 10:23

Hollywood stars. Professional athletes. CEO's. The rich and the famous. And while money isn't itself a bad thing, the love of money is. Jesus says that rich people usually have serious difficulty in developing relationships with God. This is because having money makes us feel important, self-sufficient and invincible: that we don't need God. Blessed are the poor, for theirs is the kingdom of heaven. Do you need God? Are you blessed?

Intro to Luke

Legend has it that, in addition to being a Greek physician, an avid historian and an effective missionary, Luke was the world's first iconographer, or painter of sacred people.

In fact, ancient sources suggest that, while Luke was conducting a live personal interview with Mary, Jesus' mother, for his upcoming biography of the life of Christ, he asked her if she would mind sitting perfectly still for a few more hours (or days) while he captured her on canvas.

Apparently, she didn't. And he did.

So pervasive was the belief in **Luke the Painter** that besides being honored as patron saint of physicians and surgeons, Luke was venerated as champion and protector of artists.

And sculptors. And stained-glass workers. And goldsmiths and glass blowers. And lace makers, and notaries public, and brewers. And butchers. And bookbinders. And bachelors.

Makes perfect sense to me (really?).

Miraculously, Luke's original painting of Mary survives to this day, or so its owners allege, hanging on a lonely sanctuary wall in a basilica in Spain. Oddly, dozens of other cathedrals also claim that they too have an original Luke Madonna in their collections of religious art in far-flung places like India, Egypt, Rome, Germany and Venice (makes one wonder).

But whether Luke ever put oil to canvas or not, he was clearly a gifted artist when it came to painting with words—so much so that the French scholar Renan called Luke's Gospel, "The most beautiful book ever written."

If you love gorgeous word pictures, your upcoming visit to Luke's narrative will be a special treat. It will be like taking an exclusive, professionally guided tour of Luke's own extensive art gallery. So as you enter, get your camera ready—the good doctor's breath-taking artwork will be hanging everywhere.

Luke's theme:

God's man thrives

Luke

Writer	Luke
Date Written	AD 64
Place Written	Greece
Recipient	Theophilus, a Greek
Theme	God's man thrives

And Jesus increased in wisdom and stature, and in favor with God and men. —Luke 2:52

The third of the four living creatures in Revelation has the face of a man. This *person* can be seen to correspond with the Christ of our third Gospel where Luke throws the rich tapestry of Jesus' humanity on center stage.

To Luke's intended audience, it was not so much Christ's ruling authority or his tireless work that mattered most. Rather, the Greeks were looking for the Utopian man.

"The Greeks attempted to perfect humanity and to develop the perfect man," says J. Vernon McGee, in his commentary on Luke. In their culture, beauty, wisdom and intelligence were highly sought after. In their writings, sculptures and mythology, they idealized human beings.

"The Greeks made their gods in the likeness of men," says McGee. "The magnificent statues of Apollo, Venus, Athena and Diana… deified man with his noble qualities… So it was to this Greek mind that Luke wrote. He presented Jesus Christ as the perfect man, the universal man, the very person the Greeks were looking for."

To this end, Luke carefully assembled the details of Jesus' life that displayed his perfectly balanced humanity, showing his readers the Person who supremely honored God and deeply cared about people.

"Whereas the emphasis in Matthew is on what Jesus **said**, and in Mark on what Jesus **did**," explains Bible teacher Sidlow Baxter, "here in Luke it is rather on **Jesus Himself**… Luke gives equal space to our Lord's deeds and words, so that neither is emphasized above the other, and both equally reflect back on the Wonder-Man Himself." Luke neatly summarized all of this for us in one simple verse found at the top of this page. In three words, God's man thrives.

Why this book was written

In his opening sentence, Luke tells us why he wrote his book:

> "Many people have set out to write accounts about the events that have been fulfilled among us. They used the eyewitness reports circulating among us from the early disciples. Having **carefully investigated everything** from the beginning, I also have decided to write a **careful account** for you, **most honorable** Theophilus, so you can be certain of the truth of everything you were taught."   **Luke 1:1-4**

"This prologue precisely resembles those of the great Greek historians, particularly Herodotus and Thucydides," comments Frederic Godet, the great Swiss theologian of the 1870's. "There is nothing like it in the other two synoptics," (that is, Matthew and Mark).

As a skilled historian, and based on an exhaustive investigation of the facts, Luke believed that he knew more about Jesus' life than others who had previously attempted to write biographies. This is why he felt qualified to write this book.

That he had **carefully investigated everything** speaks to thoroughness. Luke's writing is characterized by minute attention to detail. That he wrote a **careful account** is a Greek way of saying that his book is chronological.

According to the prologue, Luke dedicated his book to a man named Theophilus, who may have asked him to write it and as a patron, would have paid him handsomely to do so. Though no one knows for sure who Theophilus was, his **most honorable** title indicates that he was probably a high-ranking government official who was eager to confirm what he had previously learned about Jesus.

Yet, besides these things, since Luke was a Greek Christian missionary and pastor, his real motivation for the book may have come from his own deep-felt desire to broadcast the message of God's salvation across the Greek world.

A brief outline of the book

Luke's Gospel has five parts. By far the book's largest part is its 11-chapter road trip, or *travelogue*, as some call it, which starts at the end of chapter nine and runs all the way to the middle of the 19th chapter.

This large section (407 verses) dominates the book. It documents Jesus' work and teaching during the last six months of his life, as he travels from Galilee to Jerusalem, where he will be crucified. It also contains 10 of Luke's 11 masterpiece parables.

	Chapters
Birth—the perfect man is born—and introduced	1-4
Work—he speaks, works, and lives—all perfectly	5-9
Road trip—he marches toward his destiny in Jerusalem	9-19
Passion—he successfully completes his mission	20-23
Ascension—he ascends to heaven to help us from above	24

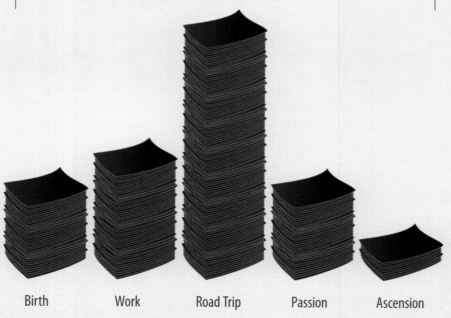

Birth   Work   Road Trip   Passion   Ascension

Verses that demonstrate Jesus' perfect humanity

How would a perfect person act? What would he say? What would he do? Luke's book suggests that he would dedicate his life to loving God and taking care of his fellow human beings. Just like Jesus did.

"The Savior—yes, the Messiah, the Lord—has been born today in Bethlehem." **Luke 2:11**

"The Spirit of the Lord… has anointed me to bring Good News to the poor." **4:18**

"He has sent me to proclaim that captives will be released." **4:18**

"That the blind will see, that the oppressed be set free." **4:18**

When the Lord saw her, his heart overflowed with compassion. **7:13**

When he saw the man, he felt compassion for him. **10:33**

Filled with love and compassion, he ran to his son, embraced him and kissed him. **15:20**

Then Jesus called for the children… "Let the children come to me." **18:16**

As… Jesus saw the city ahead, he began to weep. **19:41**

Jesus said, "Father, forgive them, for they don't know what they are doing." **23:34**

And Jesus replied, "I assure you, today you will be with me in paradise." **23:43**

The Roman officer… said, "Surely this man was innocent." **23:47**

How to navigate Luke

1. **Read Luke straight through**

   Luke's book is written chronologically. You should read it straight through, beginning to end. And as you read, remember that Luke is presenting Jesus to his Greek audience as God's thriving man.

2. **Study Luke's 11 masterpiece parables**

   Luke recorded Jesus' most famous and impactful parables. The following parables can be found only in Luke. Study them one by one:

   a. the two debtors— **Luke 7:41-43**

   b. the good Samaritan—**10:30-37**

   c. the stubborn friend—**11:5-8**

   d. the rich fool—**12:16-21**

   e. the barren fig tree—**13:6-9**

   f. the lost coin—**15:8-10**

   g. the prodigal son—**15:11-32**

   h. the unjust steward—**16:1-12**

   i. the rich man and Lazarus—**16:19-31**

   j. the persistent widow—**18:1-18**

   k. the Pharisee and the tax collector—**18:9-14**

3. **Read Jesus' prayers**

   Luke includes nine of Jesus' prayers—more than any other Gospel. Seven are unique to this book.

   a. during his baptism—**3:21**   *(only in Luke)*

   b. before challenging opponents—**5:15-16**   *(only in Luke)*

   c. before selecting the Twelve—**6:12**   *(only in Luke)*

   d. before predicting his crucifixion—**9:18-22**   *(only in Luke)*

   e. during his transfiguration—**9:29**   *(only in Luke)*

   f. after seventy disciples returned—**10:17-21**

   g. before teaching the Lord's Prayer—**11:1**   *(only in Luke)*

   h. in the garden of Gethsemane—**22:39-46**

   i. on the cross for forgiveness—**23:34,46**   *(only in Luke)*

Unique things about Luke

Did you know...

Luke features Mary's song—the Magnificat

In the opening chapter of his Gospel, Luke presents Mary's song, also known as the Magnificat—the first word of the song's Latin translation. When Mary speaks this inspired hymn of praise to her cousin Elizabeth during the days of her divine pregnancy, her soul "magnifies the Lord" for what he has done for her. Christians the world over revere this song as one of the most beautiful passages of the Bible (Luke 1:46-55).

Luke has shepherds, angels and baby Jesus

Only Luke tells the story of the shepherds who are visited by an angel, and who, in turn, pay a visit to Jesus in the manger. And only Luke paints the sky with millions of angels, who are seen praising God loudly at the birth of the Savior.

Luke's genealogy runs backwards

Only Matthew and Luke provide genealogies of Jesus. Mark and John do not. Matthew's begins at Abraham and comes forward to Jesus—it is Mary's lineage—and proves that Jesus is a descendant of Abraham. Luke's starts with Jesus and runs backwards, all the way to Adam—it is Joseph's lineage—and proves that Jesus is the Savior of *all* mankind.

Women rule

Luke goes out of his way to showcase women in his narrative. He opens the book by highlighting the critical roles of Mary, Elizabeth and Anna in the divine story of Jesus' birth and continues to introduce us to women of faith through the rest of the book. Ironically, at Jesus' arrest and crucifixion, while the men run panic-stricken for cover, the women stand firm.

Recap

- Think of Luke as an artist who paints with words. His "most beautiful book ever written" is like a famous art gallery, full of masterpieces.

- The story of Jesus, for Luke, is the story of God's perfect man.

- Keep In mind that the longest part of Luke is an 11-chapter road trip (chapters 9-19) chronicling events which took place in the final six months of Jesus' ministry.

Read it!

- Read Luke now. At a casual reading pace, total reading time is 2 hours and 20 minutes. You can finish it in seven 20-minute sessions..

Self-study / Group discussion questions

- What is it about the book of Luke that might cause some to regard it as "the most beautiful book ever written?"

- Luke spends 11 of his 24 chapters describing Jesus' final road trip, even though it covers only six months of Jesus' ministry. What might have caused Luke to want to spend so much time reporting on this period of time?

- Luke presents Jesus to his readers as the perfect human being. What would a perfect human be like? Put into words your description of a *perfect human*. In what ways do you desire to be more complete, whole and mature?

Insights that we can apply today

"The Son of Man came to seek and save those who are lost."

—Luke 19:10

Jesus came to find the lost, people like you and me who are spiritually disoriented, off track, senseless. And when he finds us, he brings us back to God, so that he can give us eternal life. The Bible says that we all, like sheep, have gone astray. Jesus wants to find you. Are you lost? Or found?

Intro to John

The Gospel of John is the last of the four biographies of Christ in the New Testament. And if Matthew is like five shiny skyscrapers, Mark, a rock star, and Luke, a popular art gallery, then John has to be the world's oldest continuously operating restaurant. For 2,000 years it has been *the* eatery of choice for millions of tired and hungry people.

According to a well-established French legend, the word *restaurant* first came into popular usage in Paris in 1765 when a food entrepreneur by the name of Boulanger splashed the word *restaurer* (*restoratives* in English) across the front of his newly opened soup kitchen.

"Eating a hearty bowl of my sheep feet in white cream sauce," advertised Boulanger, "will quickly 'restore' your vim and vigor." And whether or not it ever did, the word *restaurant* stuck.

Today, countless restaurants from Seattle to Shanghai serve billions of paying customers sandwiches, snails, sea bass and everything else under the sun. But not one of them can dish up a plateful of the divine, nourishing and soul-satisfying food that Chef John prepares.

Only John serves **the bread of life** to his clientele, the heavenly food that came down to earth to satisfy spiritual appetites everywhere. One bite of the Word of God, promises Jesus in John's Gospel, and your deepest hunger will be filled. And you will live forever!

William Barclay would agree. Barclay, a well-respected Scottish minister and university professor, became a household name in 1954 when his *Daily Study Bible Series* was first published. The immensely popular original English edition sold more than five million copies. And it's still in print today.

"For many Christians," says Barclay, "the Gospel of John is the most precious book in the New Testament. It is the book on which above all they **feed** their minds, and **nourish** their hearts, and in which they **rest** their souls."

Welcome to John's place. Enjoy.

John's theme:
Heaven's eagle soars

John

Writer	John
Date Written	AD 80
Place Written	Ephesus
Recipients	New Christians and God-seekers
Theme	Heaven's eagle soars

"I am the resurrection and the life."   —John 11:25

The fourth living creature in Revelation is the eagle, a magnificent raptor that is uniquely qualified to represent Jesus in John. Whereas the lion, the ox and the man all share terra firma as their natural habitat, the eagle soars heavenward, high above it all, free as a bird. No one can bring him down.

In similar fashion, while Matthew, Mark and Luke all focus their camera lenses on Jesus the Man, John reminds us, above all else, that Jesus is God, divine and transcendent.

As you might expect, eagle metaphors abound in the Bible. And they are fabulous illustrations of God's attributes. Here's one: immediately after God delivered the children of Israel from 400 years of slavery, He said to them, "You have seen what I did to the Egyptians. You know how I carried you on eagles' wings and brought you to myself" (Exodus 19:4).

In this verse, "the eagles' wings are figurative," say C.F. Keil and Franz Delitzsch, world-renowned Old Testament scholars, "and denote the strong and loving care of God." This same strong and loving care of God is the message of John's Gospel, made tangible in the person of Jesus Christ: "For God loved the world so much that he gave his one and only Son…" (John 3:16).

Here's another one: eagles soar. Isaiah says, "Those who trust in the Lord will find new strength. They will soar high on wings like eagles" (Isaiah 40:31).

In the language of John's day, these transcendent ones are those who believe in Jesus. "I am the resurrection and the life," Jesus says. "Everyone who lives in me and believes in me will never die" (John 11:25-26).

In her book, *Just Give Me Jesus,* Anne Graham Lotz's haunting description of Jesus calls to mind an image of a lone eagle circling high above the mountains in the moonlight. Says Anne, "He is unparalleled, and He is unprecedented. He stands in the solitude of Himself."

Why this book was written

Sometime around AD 80, during his latter years, John, a former fisherman and "the disciple whom Jesus loved," took up residence in Ephesus, a city on the western seacoast of a country known today as Turkey. There, he took care of a group of churches, clustered within 50 miles of each other, which had been started years earlier by the Apostle Paul.

As a young Galilean disciple, John's brash, intense and somewhat vengeful personality had earned him the nickname "Son of Thunder." But with the passage of time, John had mellowed considerably: these days he mostly talked about "God's love."

As was his custom, this oldest surviving Apostle traveled among the churches preaching and teaching the things that he had seen and heard firsthand when Jesus was still on the planet.

Over time, church leaders realized that much of what they were hearing from John was not included in the books about Jesus that had already been written by Matthew, Mark and Luke. They also knew that John wouldn't be around forever.

So one day, they approached John and encouraged him to write down his own account of the life of Christ to document the events, conversations and details that were not recorded elsewhere. John gladly complied.

Most likely, as John composed his biography, he spread out copies of the other three Gospels in front of him. Then, as he identified gaps in their accounts, he was inspired to select appropriate stories to fill them. But John also had a higher purpose in mind: he wanted people to have eternal life and to understand Jesus from a heavenly, divine perspective.

"The disciples saw Jesus do many other miraculous signs," wrote John, "in addition to the ones recorded in this book. But these are written so that you may continue to believe that Jesus is the Messiah, the Son of God, and that by believing in him you will have life by the power of his name" (John 20:30-31).

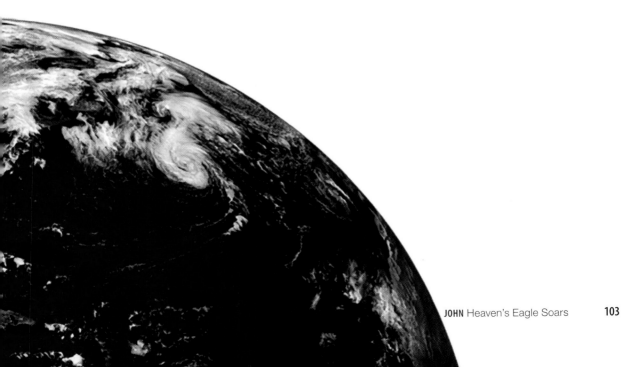

A brief outline of the book

The simplest way to think about the structure of John's book is to picture three large blocks of text with an introduction inserted in front and a P.S. tacked onto the back end.

The first major section is Jesus' public ministry, in which John presents a series of Jesus' encounters with individuals. The second part records the private talks Jesus had with his closest disciples on the night before he died on the cross. And the third gives us John's version of Jesus' *passion*: his arrest, crucifixion, death and resurrection.

	Chapters
Heaven's eagle is introduced—Jesus, the God-man	1
Public ministry—working with people	2-12
Private talks—training his disciples	13-17
Passion—accomplishing his mission	18-20
Heaven's eagle rises and soars	21

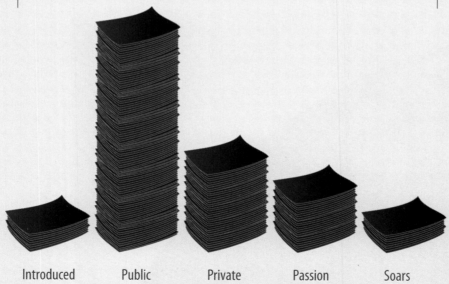

| Introduced | Public | Private | Passion | Soars |

Verses that show that Jesus is God and came to give us eternal life

In his book, John makes two points. The first: that Jesus is God—the divine God-man. The following verses support this point.

> In the beginning the Word already existed. The Word was with God, and was God. **John 1:1**

> So the Word became human and made his home among us. **1:14**

> The one and only Son is himself God. He has revealed… God to us. **1:18**

> "My Lord and my God!" Thomas exclaimed. **20:28**

The second point is that Jesus, God's Son, came to give people eternal life. The following verses support this point.

> The Word gave life to everything that was created and his life brought light to everyone. **1:4**

> But to all who believed him and accepted him, he gave the right to become children of God. **1:12**

> Everyone who believes in him will not perish but have eternal life. **3:16**

> "Those who listen to my message and believe in God who sent me have eternal life." **5:24**

> "I am the gate for the sheep… My purpose is to give them a rich and satisfying life." **10:6,10**

> "I give them eternal life, and they will never perish." **10:28**

> "Everyone who lives in me and believes in me will never die." **11:26**

> "I am the way, the truth, and the life. No one can come to the Father except through me". **14:6**

How to navigate John

1. **Read John straight through**

    Because of John's warm and inviting writing style, the book of John is the most approachable book in the New Testament. The book's simple, straightforward language and its encouraging message make it an ideal first book for newer Bible readers to read. But this doesn't mean that the book is shallow. It also has great depths to dive into and explore.

2. **Be on the lookout for the seven** *"I ams"*

    Only John captures the "I am" language Jesus used to describe himself. Using this language, Jesus created seven metaphors to give us tangible images of mysterious spiritual things.

    a. *I am* the bread of life—**6:35**
    b. *I am* the light of the world—**8:12**
    c. *I am* the door to salvation—**10:9**
    d. *I am* the good shepherd—**10:11**
    e. *I am* the resurrection and the life—**11:25**
    f. *I am* the way, the truth, and the life—**14:6**
    g. *I am* the vine—**15:5**

3. **Pay attention to Jesus' seven "signs"**

    John records seven of Jesus' miracles, which he calls *signs*. Five of them are unique to John. Watch for them as you read the book. Here they are:

    a. changing water into wine—**2:1-11**   *(only in John)*
    b. healing a royal official's son—**5:15-16**   *(only in John)*
    c. healing an impotent man—**5:1-9**   *(only in John)*
    d. feeding 10,000 people—**6:1-5**
    e. walking on water—**6:16-25**
    f. giving sight to the man born blind—**9:1-41** *(only in John)*
    g. raising Lazarus from the dead—**11:1-44**   *(only in John)*

Unique things about John

Did you know. . .

John uses the word *believe* nearly 100 times in his book

One of John's objectives in writing his book was to strengthen the believers' faith. This is why he used the word *believe* time and time again. Believers believe: that's what they do. And John encourages us to do more of it.

There are no parables in John—at all

The Gospels include over 30 of Jesus' parables. But none of them can be found in John. They didn't suit his purposes. Besides, the other three Gospel writers had done a great job of documenting them.

John's Jesus prefers personal conversations

John recorded a number of conversations that Jesus had with individuals. Among these are his one-on-ones with Nicodemus (chapter three), the Samaritan woman (chapter four), the royal official (chapter four), the lame man at the pool of Bethesda (chapter five), Thomas (chapter 20) and many others. No other Gospel includes these conversations.

Jesus was a writer and a chef

John documents the only occasion in the Bible where Jesus wrote anything. In chapter eight, Jesus stooped down and wrote in the dust with his finger. Nobody knows what he wrote: the Bible doesn't tell us. And in chapter 21, John records the only time in the Bible where Jesus prepared food. One morning, he cooked breakfast on the beach for his disciples. That day, roasted fish on toast was on the menu.

Recap

- Think of the book of John as a fabulous restaurant that is always open. Here Jesus serves *the bread of life* to people from all over the world.

- Visualize Jesus in John's book as heaven's eagle, soaring high above the earth, rising above all human challenges and circumstances.

- Picture the outline of John's book as three large pieces: Jesus' public ministry, his private talks and his passion.

Read it!

- Read John now. At a casual reading pace, total reading time is 1 hour and 40 minutes. You can finish it in five 20-minute sessions.

Self-study / Group discussion questions

- In what ways is the Gospel of John different from Matthew, Mark and Luke? What is it about John's book that makes it "the most precious book in the New Testament?"

- What are the two points John is making in his book? Why are these important?

- God's lion roars. God's ox dies. God's man thrives. Heaven's eagle soars. Which of these themes of the four Gospels speaks to you the most? Why?

Insights that we can apply today

"My sheep hear my voice... and they follow me." —John 10:27

For Christ followers, the Lord is our Shepherd, and we are his sheep. He is our leader, and we are his followers. He is the speaker, and we are supposed to be the listeners. But when you pray, who does most of the talking, you or God? Don't you think that the Lord has something he wants to say to you? Why not stop and try to listen for his voice a little more?

History

Intro to Acts

In his first book, Luke's narrative of Christ's life ends as Jesus, in his newly resurrected body, says goodbye to his friends and followers and lifts off from the Mount of Olives for the first leg of his round trip to heaven.

Now in his second volume, the book of Acts, Luke picks up the action where he left off as Jesus, having reached heaven, sends the Spirit of God back down to the earth. The Spirit, now pictured by Luke in pyrotechnic form, begins spreading like **wildfire**.

And while you don't have to be a rocket scientist to understand this book, it would help a great deal if you were a fire scientist. Someone like, well, like Richard C. Rothermel, for instance.

Dick Rothermel, as his closest friends know him, is one of the world's leading fire behaviorists. He studies fires in order to predict their behaviors. Dick walked onto the world's stage in 1972. That was the year when, after months of painstaking research at the Fire Sciences Lab of the United States Forest Service in Missoula, Montana, Dick and his team developed the following mathematical equation to predict how fast forest fires spread. It still drives the models fire fighters use to outfox forest fires today.

$$R = I_R \, \xi \, (1 + \Phi_w + \Phi_s) \, / \, \rho \, n \, e \, Qig$$

To the uninitiated, this formula looks highly complex. But fire scientists would tell you that it's really quite simple. All one needs to do, they might confidently assert, is to enter calculations for the fire reaction intensity of the adjacent fuel particles into the computer, along with a dimensionless wind effect multiplier, the amount of oven dry fuel per cubic foot of fuel bed, a terrain slope factor, a pre-ignition heat requirement factor and out pops the fire's estimated speed (R).

Or, you could simply turn to the bone weary firefighter on your left and yell over that deafening crackling noise, "This here blaze is spreading like wildfire."

Either way, by the time the Spirit of God had lit up the hearts of Jesus' disciples in Acts chapter two, it was already too late. This wildfire would run unabated for the next 26 chapters, spreading 1,603 miles from Jerusalem to Rome, joyfully consuming everything in its path.

Acts' theme:

The Spirit spreads like wildfire

Acts

Writer	Luke
Date written	AD 65
Place written	Rome
Recipient	Theophilus
Theme	The Spirit spreads like wildfire

> Suddenly, there was a sound from heaven like the roaring of a mighty windstorm... Then, what looked like flames... of fire appeared and settled on each of them. —Acts 2:2-3

To some people, the book of Acts is a primer of the Christian church and its practices: a blueprint of its birth, its growth and its methods. The book takes us back to where it all began and shows us how to do church.

To others, it is the story of Peter and Paul, the two greatest preachers of all time, that is, besides Jesus. In the first half of the book, we see Peter boldly evangelizing the Jewish world in Palestine and beyond. In the second, we follow Paul as he travels tirelessly across Asia Minor and Europe converting droves of unbelieving pagans along the way.

But there's another way to think about Acts that's different from a church how-to manual or a book of Christian history. Visualize the book as fire: raging, blazing, unpredictable fire.

Fire, in the Old Testament, symbolized God's presence. When God called Moses to rescue the Israelites out of bondage in Egypt, he spoke to him, quite unexpectedly, from the midst of a *burning* bush, on fire but not consumed. Moses was asked to take off his shoes because the ground was holy; and the ground was holy because God was present.

And while fire has a similar New Testament meaning, this time it's the Holy Spirit who's aflame, and his fire is swiftly spreading, one person to another. "Through the Spirit, some of the creative power of God Himself comes from heaven to earth and does its work there," says Tom Wright, a noted Bible scholar. "What the Spirit will do when He comes is anybody's guess. Be prepared for wind and fire, for some drastic spring-cleaning of the dusty and cold rooms of your life."

Why this book was written

Luke had dedicated his first book to a government official by the name of Theophilus to confirm his faith in Jesus as the Messiah. Now in his sequel, written for the benefit of the same person, Luke's goal was to deepen his friend's beliefs.

Luke accomplished this objective by documenting the rapid expansion of Christianity across the Roman world. In telling this story, he demonstrated how God's Spirit, working through believers, powerfully impacted society. And on an individual level he illustrated how faith in Jesus had changed people, and ultimately their communities, for the better.

Luke wanted to present Christianity in a positive light, for, to many members of the ruling class, *the Way*, as New Testament believers were commonly known at the time, had developed quite a bad reputation. Most people thought of Christians as a splinter group within the Jewish religion. And as repeated violent Jewish disturbances broke out across the empire, though they were unrelated to the Way, Roman attitudes towards Christians soured.

Christians were considered troublemakers.

One way Luke overcame this bad press was to document the joyous effect the early churches had on their local communities. The Christians in Jerusalem, Luke argued, were fabulous neighbors. They "shared their meals with great joy and generosity—all the while praising God and enjoying the goodwill of all the people" (Acts 2:46-47). What more could you ask for?

At the end of the book, Luke elevated the perception of the Christian movement further by heralding the arrival of Paul, its greatest apostle, at Rome, the capital of the empire.

The preaching of Christ had made it to center stage.

A brief outline of the book

Structurally, Acts has two sections: the first section showcases Peter's ministry—the second, Paul's. Peter's ministry begins in chapter one in the city of Jerusalem and from there fans out across Palestine. Paul's starts in Antioch in neighboring Syria and, through a series of well-documented journeys, spreads all the way to Rome.

	Chapters
Peter's ministry	
Peter working in Jerusalem	1-7
Peter working beyond Jerusalem	8-12
Paul's ministry	
Paul's first journey—Antioch to Galatia	13-15
Paul's second journey—Antioch to Greece	16-18
Paul's third journey—Antioch to Ephesus and Greece	19-20
Paul's voyage from Palestine to Rome	21-28

Peter's ministry   Paul's ministry

Verses that illustrate the Spirit spreading like wildfire

Luke does a great job of describing the growth of the Christian church by inserting **summary verses** here and there along the way. These verses quantify the numbers of new converts coming into churches through the efforts of Peter, Paul and the Holy Spirit. They also add momentum to the story.

"And you will be my witnesses, telling people about me everywhere." **Acts 1:8**

And everyone present was filled with the Holy Spirit and began speaking in other languages. **2:4**

Those who believed… were… added to the church that day—about 3,000 in all. **2:41**

And each day the Lord added to their fellowship those who were being saved. **2:47**

So the number of believers totaled about 5,000 men, not counting women and children. **4:4**

So God's message continued to spread. The number of believers greatly increased. **6:7**

The church had peace… became stronger… it also grew in numbers. **9:31**

A large number of these Gentiles believed and turned to the Lord. **11:21**

So the churches were strengthened in their faith and grew larger every day. **16:5**

Some of the Jews joined Paul and Silas… along with many God-fearing Greek men. **17:4**

That ended Paul's discussion with them… but some joined him and became believers. **18:34**

So the message about the Lord spread widely and had a powerful effect. **19:20**

How to navigate Acts

1. **Read Acts straight through**

   Luke is a master storyteller. His book of Acts is a factual, historical account, yet it reads like a novel. Make it a point to read it straight through, beginning to end. You might not be able to put it down.

2. **Notice people, places and things**

   As you read Acts, you will be introduced to over 100 different people. Luke will also be taking you to dozens of new places, exposing you to many cultural groups. It would be informative and fun to create lists of people and places as you read. Grab your pen!

3. **Study the *Acts 2* model church**

   The first church on earth was the church in Jerusalem. In Acts 2:42-47, Luke paints a brief but vivid picture of the wonderful, attractive, joyful, buoyant, empowered, self-sacrificial, unified lives of the early Christians who lived this church life. It is a model for the rest of us.

Unique things about Acts

Did you know...

The Spirit is mentioned over 50 times in Acts

Though the work of Peter and Paul is showcased in this book, God's Spirit is the real star of the show. Through each of the book's 28 chapters, the Spirit is constantly moving and shaking as he fills, speaks, empowers, restores, directs, prohibits, baptizes, urges, comforts, rejoices and sanctifies.

There are three *we* sections

Luke not only wrote this book, he participated in it too. Luke accompanied Paul on parts of the journeys he recorded in the book. In fact, on three occasions, as Luke joined the party, the narrative changed from reporting what *they* did to telling what *we* did. These *we* sections, as they're commonly known, are: Acts 16:10-18, 20:6-21:17 and 27:1-28:16.

Paul tells his story three times

In Acts chapter nine, Luke vividly describes Paul's dramatic, face-to-face encounter with Jesus on the road to Damascus. Later in the book, Paul re-tells the same story on two different occasions (Acts 22:1-21 and 26:1-23). Is Luke being intentional in recording all three? You bet he is.

It's a fantastic sea story

In Acts 27, Luke tells the gripping story of Paul's spectacular, two-thousand-mile voyage across the Mediterranean Sea. As a passenger on this ill-timed crossing from Palestine to Rome, Luke experienced it all, including a two-week-long typhoon, an awful shipwreck and three months stranded on the island of Malta. R.C.H. Lenski, a well-known Lutheran Bible scholar, calls this story, "The most perfect account of an ancient sea voyage ever penned."

Recap

- When you think of the book of Acts, picture a raging wildfire spreading out of control across the face of the earth. It's the Spirit of God fanning out in all directions.

- As you read Acts, notice the rapid increase in the number of believers being added to the church. The Christian movement is taking off.

- Remember that Acts is organized in two major sections: Peter's ministry (chapters 1-12) and Paul's ministry (chapters 13-28).

Read it!

- Read Acts now. At a casual reading pace, total reading time is 2 hours and 20 minutes. You can finish it in seven 20-minute sessions.

Self-study / Group discussion questions

- Why did Luke write this book? What were his objectives and motivations? Why was this an important book to write?

- In your mind, picture a raging wildfire, burning unabated in a remote, unpopulated area. Why are this compelling visual image and "The Spirit spreads like wildfire" appropriate themes for Acts?

- Though Luke develops his historical account through the ministries of Peter and Paul, many believe that God's Spirit is the real *star* of this book. Why is that?

Insights that we can apply today

Paul and Silas have caused trouble all over the world... and now they are here disturbing our city too. —Acts 17:6

The early Christians were world-changers. Wherever they went, by the power of the Holy Spirit, they turned things right side up. They brought hope to the poor. Strength to the weak. Joy to the sad. Spiritual freedom to the oppressed. Just like Jesus did. And it's no different today. In Christ, we have the power to change the world. What's keeping us from doing so?

Paul's Travels

1. First Journey

Elapsed Time   Two years (AD 45-47)
Places   Cyprus and Galatia

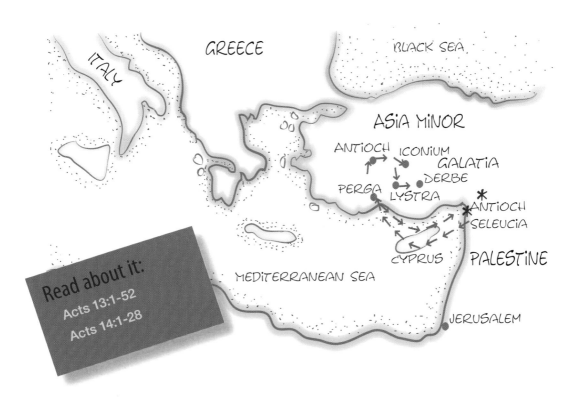

Read about it:
Acts 13:1-52
Acts 14:1-28

0   100   200

MILES

Highlights

First Journey

This is the story of Paul's travels. It starts in Acts chapter eight. Here, Luke introduces us to Saul, an angry, young, ambitious, highly-educated, self-styled Jewish vigilante, whose favorite hobby is hunting down deviant Jews and throttling them for abandoning their Hebrew faith to become Christians.

Ironically, in Acts chapter nine it's Saul himself who is brought to faith in Christ, in most dramatic fashion, when Jesus Himself ambushes him on the road to Damascus, knocking him down, flat on his back.

Now, some 10 years of eye-popping, Jesus-taught faith lessons later, Saul's transformative Christian education approaches completion as he prepares himself to respond to God's call on his life. His mission: to carry his Master's message of forgiveness and everlasting life to people who live in the vast Roman Empire outside the borders of Palestine.

Joined by Barnabas, a fellow Bible teacher and missionary, and Mark, a young apprentice, Saul (whose Roman name is Paul), leaves his home in Antioch, by ship and on foot, bound for the island of Cyprus and beyond.

Over the next two years Paul's party travels over 500 miles, visiting synagogue after synagogue in city after city, persuading their scattered Jewish countrymen, and anyone else who will listen, that Jesus is the long-awaited Savior of the world. Many hundreds believe. But the zealous Jews don't. Instead, they become Paul's archenemies, who in turn take great pleasure in hunting *him* down and throttling him, as frequently as possible.

Early on in the trip, for some still unknown reason, Mark unexpectedly decides that he has had quite enough adventure for one outing. After bidding Paul and Barnabas adieu, he heads home to Jerusalem, leaving his spiritual mentors to fend for themselves. Adding insult to injury is the fact that Barnabas is Mark's uncle, the one who persuaded Paul to take him along in the first place.

Some months later, after Paul and Barnabas wrap up their gospel preaching work in the town of Derbe, they turn around, retrace their steps and head for the coast. There they jump a freighter and sail home to Syria.

Paul's Travels

2. Second Journey

Elapsed Time   Three years (AD 50-52)
Places   Galatia, Asia Minor and Greece

Read about it:
Acts 15:36-41
Acts 16:1-40
Acts 17:1-34
Acts 18:1-22

0   100   200
MILES

Highlights

Second Journey

Paul and Barnabas spend the next two years working side by side in Antioch, preaching and teaching the Word of God. Then one day, from out of the blue, Paul turns to his partner, and says, "Hey Barnabas, I've been thinking. How about we go back and visit the believers in all the places where we preached during our first road trip? I'm dying to know how they're doing."

Barnabas thinks this is a fabulous idea but insists that they take his nephew Mark along with them (again).

"Over my dead body," snaps Paul. "I've never met such a flaky guy. Last time, he completely bailed out on us. It's NOT going to happen!"

But Barnabas stands firm—he has his reasons. And so does Paul. Soon a debate over principles ignites and becomes quite heated. And when the dust finally settles, these two long time ministry partners agree to disagree and go their separate ways.

Barnabas takes Mark and sails southwest to Cyprus. Paul chooses Silas as his new companion and heads north, over the mountains, to Derbe and Lystra. There they meet an eager Christian teenager named Timothy who joins them, and the three travel northwest through Asia Minor.

Over the next 20 years, Paul becomes the greatest missionary of all time. He writes 13 books of the Bible. Mark grows up, reconciles with Paul and becomes his highly valued co-worker. He also writes the Gospel of Mark. Timothy matures into Paul's much-cherished *son in the faith*. Two New Testament letters bear his name. Barnabas is not heard from again.

During this second missionary journey, Paul's threesome brings the good news of Jesus Christ to people in cities across Asia and Europe, as they log 1,800 miles over three years. Along the way, they're constantly hounded by irate Jewish fanatics bent on killing them. Undaunted, and with God's help, they leave vibrant Christian congregations in their wake, founding churches in Philippi, Thessalonica, Berea, Corinth and elsewhere.

Paul remains in Corinth 18 months. There he writes the first two of his biblical letters, known today as **1 Thessalonians** and **2 Thessalonians**.

Paul's Travels

3. Third Journey

Elapsed Time Four years (AD 55-60)
Places Galatia, Asia Minor and Greece

GREECE
BLACK SEA
ITALY
PHILIPPI
THESSALONICA NEAPOLIS
BEREA
ASIA MINOR
TROAS
ANTIOCH ICONIUM
ATHENS GALATIA
CORINTH EPHESUS DERBE
LYSTRA TARSUS
RHODES *ANTIOCH
CYPRUS PALESTINE
MEDITERRANEAN SEA TYRE
CAESAREA
*JERUSALEM

Read about it:
Acts 18:23-28
Acts 19:1-41
Acts 20:1-37
Acts 21:1-15

0   100   200
MILES

Highlights

Third Journey

After a short season of R & R at home in Antioch, Paul once again takes to the open road and journeys westward, visiting friends in churches across the provinces of Asia Minor. Soon, he reaches Ephesus, the region's most important city, located on the west coast of today's Turkey. A major chunk of this third journey's activity plays itself out here.

Ephesus is both the capital of the region and its major trading center. But, more importantly, it is the adopted home of the Roman goddess, Diana, complete with a spectacular temple built in her honor. This amazing edifice, the size of a football field and 50 feet high, was made entirely out of marble. It took 120 years to build and was one of the Seven Wonders of the World.

Unfortunately, the temple was destroyed in 356 BC. Yet, for centuries after its destruction, religious pilgrims the world over continue to flock to the city, both to pay homage to their great idol goddess and to purchase Diana souvenirs—take-home statues and shrines made of silver, bronze and clay.

This booming tourist trade fuels the local economy. That is, until Paul arrives in town in AD 55. During the next two years, as his idol-free Gospel gains traction with the Ephesians, a chain reaction occurs. As droves of converts abandon the idol cult to follow Jesus, sales of Diana memorabilia fall off. And as revenues deteriorate, incomes of shrine craftsmen evaporate.

With their livelihoods thus threatened, the local artisans explode, staging an uprising against Paul and his friends. Fired up by an outspoken silversmith named Demetrius, statue makers of all kinds run screaming through the streets of Ephesus creating panic in the city.

Though the City Manager intervenes to quell this huge civil disturbance before the craftsmen tear the Christians limb from limb, Paul decides that it's high time for him to leave town and moves on. During his three-year stay in Ephesus, Paul wrote two New Testament letters, **Galatians** and **1 Corinthians**. Then over the next year, as he traveled through Greece, Paul wrote **2 Corinthians** and **Romans** before returning to Palestine via Jerusalem.

Paul's Travels

4. Voyage to Rome

Elapsed Time   Two years (AD 62-64)
Places   Mediterranean and Adriatic Seas

ROME
ITALY
GREECE
BLACK SEA
ASIA MINOR
SICILY
SYRACUSE
MALTA
ADRIATIC SEA
CRETE
CYPRUS
PALESTINE
MEDITERRANEAN SEA
SIDON
CAESAREA
JERUSALEM

Read about it:
Acts 21:17-22:29
Acts 22:30-26:32
Acts 27:1-28:16

0   100   200
MILES

Highlights

Voyage to Rome

Unbeknownst to him, serious trouble is waiting for Paul when he arrives in Jerusalem, the world capital of the Jewish religion. It's been 22 years since this former Hebrew defender turned Christian and abandoned his faith. But the zealous Jews haven't forgotten. And now he's on their home turf.

Within a short time, Paul causes an uproar when he pays a visit to the Jewish temple. There, frenzied religious extremists grab him and beat him to within an inch of his life. They would have killed him outright had not the commander of the Roman garrison rushed troops onto the scene and yanked him out of the melee, just in the nick of time.

Now, in Roman hands for his own protection, and though having committed no crime, Paul is kept in various prisons for two years for political reasons. During this time, rather than facing trumped up charges at a Jewish trial in Jerusalem, Paul plays his "I'm a Roman citizen and you can't treat me this way" card and appeals his case to Caesar.

So, to Caesar Paul goes, shackled but confident, sailing off to Rome with Luke, dozens of other prisoners and a regiment of Roman soldiers on the adventure of their lives.

By the time the ill-fated voyagers finally make landfall on the south side of the island of Crete, it's already late October, when dangerous weather conditions begin to make open ocean sailing impossible. Paul strongly urges the ship's owner to winter there. But motivated by greed (time is money), he ignores Paul's advice and sails anyway (bad idea).

To make a long and thrilling sea story short, as their Alexandrian freighter skirts the south shore of Crete, a tempestuous Nor'easter grabs the vessel and drives it, out of control, southwest towards Africa. For the next 14 days, in hurricane conditions, the 276 persons on board hang on for dear life until, miraculously, they shipwreck on the island of Malta.

After everyone scrambles safely to shore, Paul coolly says, I told you so, heals the island chieftain's father, and becomes a bona fide hero. For three glorious months the Palestinian travelers enjoy marvelous island hospitality, before heading out in the Spring for Rome (aloha).

Paul's Travels

5. After His First Trial in Rome

Elapsed Time   Two years (AD 65-66?)
Places   Italy, Greece, Crete and Spain

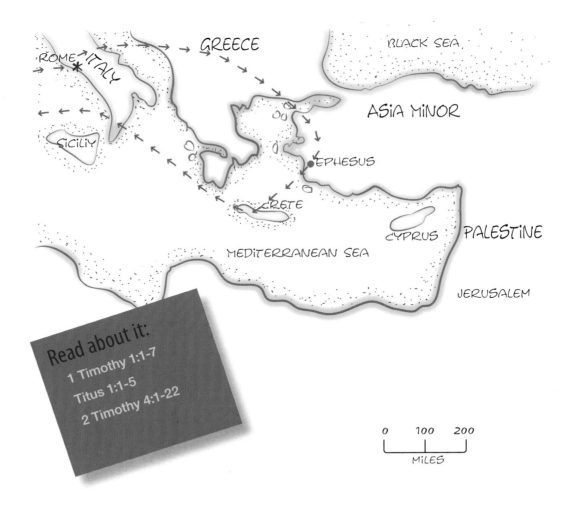

Read about it:
1 Timothy 1:1-7
Titus 1:1-5
2 Timothy 4:1-22

0   100   200
MILES

Highlights

After His First Trial in Rome

After arriving in Rome, Paul is not imprisoned like the other transported criminals, but rather awaits his hearing before Caesar in the relative comfort of his own rented home. There, he resides under constant Roman guard, free to carry on a somewhat normal existence.

Luke stays with him, as do a number of other co-workers who have come from churches in Asia and Greece to support him. And for two years life goes on. From time to time, out-of-town visitors arrive from places like Philippi or Colossae, bringing him either joyful news of God's marvelous work or thorny issues that require his God-given wisdom to solve.

In the relative quiet of this "imprisonment," God affords Paul both the luxury of time and the mental freedom to ponder deep things. So it's not surprising that Paul's most profound spiritual writings are born here, his letters of **Colossians, Ephesians** and **Philippians**. During this time he also writes his famous "you owe me one" letter to his good friend **Philemon**.

Though the book of Acts ends quite abruptly before his court date with Caesar Nero arrives, evidence from Paul's later writings suggests that he has his day in court, that he prevails, and that he is subsequently released.

Now free at last, Paul re-engages in his missionary work with the help of Timothy and Titus, his two "sons in the faith." After dropping Timothy off in Ephesus to help the church there (**1 Timothy**), and Titus in Crete to set things in order in churches on the island (**Titus**), Paul heads out, possibly to Spain, to spread Jesus' Good News to more remote parts of the globe.

Meanwhile, back in Italy's capital, trouble is brewing. Nero conveniently shifts the blame for the Fire of Rome to local Christians, and a brutal anti-Christian persecution breaks out across the Empire. With other believers, Paul is rounded up and charged, most likely, with crimes against the state.

After languishing in a deep, dark Roman dungeon for some period of time, Paul writes his farewell letter (**2 Timothy**). Then on a road outside the city, he is sent to his heavenly rest by one blow of an executioner's sword.

Paul's Letters to Churches

First Century Letters

New Testament books and letters

Following the first five books of the New Testament (four biographies and one history), the Bible shifts its literary gears and transitions from books to letters. There is a huge difference between the two. Whereas books record history and tell stories, letters communicate, sender to receiver. Books are general. Letters are specific. Books are public. Letters are private. Books are for everyone. Letters are personal.

Come to find out, of the 27 books of the New Testament, 21 are not actually books at all. They're letters, hand-written documents sent to individuals or to groups of people for specific purposes. And yet, since these 21 letters were divinely invested with spiritual content, their lessons are timeless. They continue to nourish and inspire us today.

First century letter writing

Letter writing at Paul's time was a big deal. In those days, letters were a primary means of communication. And they had their own protocols. You couldn't just throw a bunch of words down on a page and mail it—there were rules, proper ways to compose letters. And if you didn't know them, you could learn them—from teachers, from scribes, from handbooks. Or, you could pay someone, proficient in the art of letter writing, for his or her services.

Your *Aha!* moment

And now, hearing all this, what may come as a big surprise to you is that Paul followed the standard first century letter-writing conventions when he sat down and wrote his letters.

Look at the outlined format in the left-hand column on the opposite page. This is the way people in the first century structured their letters. Study this format. Then read the beginning and ending paragraphs of Corinthians, Thessalonians, Romans, Ephesians and the rest of Paul's letters.

You will see, plain as the nose on your face, that Paul is following a formula. And once you see it, the Bible will never read the same.

The format of a first century letter

Here's how a standard letter was constructed in those days. The writer would launch into the body of his letter (his purpose for writing) only after he had properly greeted and thanked everyone. Then, he would include an encouragements and instructions piece before closing with a proper four-stage sign-off. The sample letter below shows you how this formula works in practice.

I. SALUTATION

    a. Sender   Peter, your favorite son, from my college dorm room.

    b. Recipient   To my WONDERFUL dad.

    c. Greeting   Hi pops! How's it going?

II. THANKSGIVING   Thanks very much for the money you sent last week.

III. BODY   My books this semester cost $500 each.

                        Tuition is due next Monday. Room and board Tuesday.

                        I'm thinking of a road trip to Florida for Spring Break.

                        Please send more money. Sooner is better.

IV. ENCOURAGEMENTS, INSTRUCTIONS   Hang in there with your book-writing project.

                        Remember to feed my turtle.

                        Your idea of renting out my room is not a good one.

V. CLOSING

    a. Peace Wish   I hope all goes well with the Bible classes you teach.

    b. Greetings   Say hello to my friends if you run into them.

    c. Kiss   Hugs and kisses to my FAVORITE dad !

    d. Benediction   Love, Pete.

Intro to Romans

The book of Romans is the text of a letter Paul wrote to Roman Christians around AD 59. It appears first in the New Testament collection of Paul's writings for two reasons. One, it's Paul's longest letter. And two, it is a must read for all Christians. Think of it as *the* textbook of the Christian faith.

In Romans, Paul, a short, bow-legged, fifty-year-old Jewish man—who happens to be the greatest Christian teacher and missionary ever—answers some of the most frequently asked *faith* questions of all time, like: Who is God? What is salvation? What is God's plan for my future?

Speaking of *your* future, in these uncertain economic times, some people just cross their fingers and hope for the best. But if you lived in Rome at the time Paul wrote this letter, we would probably find you praying at the feet of Fortuna, the goddess of Hope, Prosperity and Increase.

In those days, **Fortuna** was portrayed as a young woman, standing next to a round ball, holding a ship's wheel in one hand and a symbol of abundance in the other. In addition to bringing you prosperity, Fortuna could steer your destiny. And the ball by her feet meant that she stood above the uncertainty of the future.

A stone statue of the goddess occupied a prominent place in a small temple in *Forum Boarium*, the cattle market in ancient Rome. Each morning a line of superstitious Romans formed outside the temple and snaked its way around the corner, packed with folks eager to ask Fortuna, in a deferential tone of voice, of course, if she would *please* give them a chunk of good luck.

Unfortunately, Fortuna was often found to be indifferent, fickle or downright mean, as statistically half of her petitioners encountered bad luck immediately following their visits. Ironically, Fortuna's temple was struck by lightning and burned—not just once, but twice (unlucky, I guess).

Back then, Paul saw things differently, writing to the Romans, "God causes everything to work together for the good of those who love God" (Romans 8:28).

Paul's way is *much* better.

Romans' theme:

Completely saved

Romans

Writer	Paul
Date written	AD 59
Place written	Corinth
Recipients	New Christians
Theme	Completely saved

> And having given them right standing, he gave them his glory.
>
> —Romans 8:30

The theme of Romans is *completely saved*, two words that suggest that there is more to salvation than meets the eye. And while some may think of Christians as nothing more than squeaky-clean do-gooders, the truth is, being saved is all about, "Who's your daddy?"

According to Romans, by an act of faith, you can experience a spiritual rebirth through which God *becomes* your Father and you *become* his child. When this happens, you are *saved* because, through this new birth, God rescues you from a place of fear, hopelessness and certain death and brings you to a place of peace, safety and eternal life.

It's much like being plucked, frightened and shivering, out of the icy North Atlantic as the unsinkable Titanic disappears behind you. This is the saved part of *completely saved*. It is an event that gives you eternal security and takes place once in your lifetime.

The *completely* part is a bit different. It suggests that as a child of God, the Spirit of God now lives in you and can empower you through all sorts of trying circumstances, in spite of your weaknesses and shortcomings. From needing patience to deal with a screaming two-year-old in the grocery store to finding courage to give a difficult speech at a business meeting, there is no end to the ways that God can *save* you every day.

Completely also means that God wants to save you from yourself, from what you are by nature, by transforming you *completely* from the inside out. In this regard, you begin your Christian life as a funky-looking caterpillar. But gradually, through the continual working of the Spirit of God, you look more like a beautiful butterfly everyday.

Why this letter was written

Paul was an expert at planting churches. As he traveled through Asia Minor and Europe, Paul shared the good news of Christ's salvation with the people he met in towns along the way, and in so doing, scattered spiritual seeds everywhere. Many of these seeds found good soil in the hearts of local residents and began to grow.

Before long, dozens of young plants had sprouted and a new church was born. Most often, Paul would then spend a few weeks in the area, nurturing these new Christians by teaching them the basics of the Christian faith, until their tender roots became firmly established.

Then, he would move on.

But with Rome, it was different. Paul had never been there, though for months he had wanted to visit the city. During a trip to Corinth, he heard the news that a number of Christian groups had formed in Rome. And though he had not established these groups, he felt compelled to reach out to them by writing them a letter.

Paul hoped the letter would accomplish two objectives. First, it would answer questions about Christian beliefs and God's salvation, instruction which would enrich new believers' minds and spirits. And second, it would introduce him to these new Christians prior to a trip he planned to make to Rome.

Paul wrote Romans around AD 59. As it turned out, he did visit Rome three years later, in AD 62, but under much different circumstances. He arrived in the city neither as a missionary nor an invited Bible teacher, but as a chained Roman prisoner, awaiting trial before Caesar Nero.

A brief outline of the letter

The easiest way to think of the structure of Romans is to imagine walking up a **flight of stairs**. Since Paul wrote Romans sequentially, the letter begins at the bottom with mankind's need for God's salvation. As Paul completes each major thought, he takes his readers one step higher until he reaches a spiritual summit at the conclusion of the letter.

	Chapters
Our need for salvation	1-3
God's way of salvation	3-4
Our new life in Christ	5-8
God's mercy despite our rejection of him	9-11
How to live your faith	12-16

Our need   God's way   Our new life   God's mercy   How to live

Verses that illustrate God's complete salvation

Romans speaks a lot about mankind's issues. The following verses highlight aspects of man's condition and the benefits of accepting God's solution.

For everyone has sinned; we all fall short of God's glorious standard. **Romans 3:23**

Since we have been made right in God's sight by faith, we have peace with God. **5:1**

God showed his great love for us by sending Christ to die for us. **5:8**

The wages of sin is death, but the free gift of God is eternal life through Christ Jesus our Lord. **6:23**

So now there is no more condemnation for those who belong to Christ Jesus. **8:1**

And the Holy Spirit helps us in our weaknesses. **8:26**

God causes everything to work together for the good of those who love God. **8:28**

If God is for us, who can ever be against us? **8:31**

Despite all these things, overwhelming victory is ours through Christ. **8:37**

And I am convinced that nothing can ever separate us from God's love. **8:38**

Let God transform you into a new person by changing the way you think. **12:2**

Now all glory to God, who is able to make you strong. **16:25**

How to navigate Romans

Become familiar with the vocabulary

Romans is full of difficult-sounding theological terms, most of which are new to our vocabulary. Before you read Romans, it's best to acquaint yourself with the following two dozen words and their meanings:

gospel of God—the good news of God's salvation

resurrection—raising up, returning from death into life

salvation—being rescued from God's judgment

righteousness—being right with God and his standards

wrath of God—God's anger against sin

judgment of God—God's promise to hold the world accountable

repentance—changing your mind regarding your sinfulness

circumcision—a Jewish rite; symbol of the Jewish people

justified—being declared "not guilty" by God

redemption—Jesus bought our lives back with his death

propitiation—appeasing God's anger against our rebellion

reconciled—made right with God by taking our offenses away

transgression—a sin, a violation of divine law

condemnation—declared legally guilty

holiness—separated from common things for a higher purpose

adoption—welcomed into God's family, positioned for inheritance

intercession—a prayer for other people

predestined—God has prepared the way ahead of us

conformed—molded into the image of Christ

glorified—revealing the true value of something hidden

confession—openly, publicly declaring faith in Christ

election—the process of believers being called by grace

transformed—changed from the inside out

sanctified—made acceptable to God

Unique things about Romans

Did you know...

Romans is righteous

The words *righteous* and *righteousness* are used over 40 times in Romans. Paul wants to be sure we know how we can be *right* with God.

Paul had lots of friends in Rome

Though he had never been to Rome, in chapter 16 Paul sent greetings to nearly 30 of his friends who lived there. Notice their interesting names:

Priscilla	Aquila	Epenetus	Mary
Andronicus	Junia	Ampliatus	Urbanus
Stachys	Apelles	Aristobulus' family	Herodion
Tryphena	Tryphosa	Persis	Rufus
Rufus' mom	Asyncritus	Phlegon	Hermas
Patrobas	Hermes	Philologus	Julia
Nereus	Nereus' sister	Olympas	

and the Lord's people from the household of Narcissus.

Benedictions, benedictions, benedictions

Benedictions are blessings, which are typically bestowed on others at the end of Christian writings or talks. Paul closes all of his New Testament letters with a benediction. But in Romans, Paul is benediction-happy and offers five different blessings: 15:13, 15:33, 16:20, 16:24 and 16:25-27.

Phoebe delivers this letter to Rome

According to Romans 16:1-2, a woman named Phoebe may have carried this letter from Corinth to Rome. Paul introduces Phoebe to his readers as a *sister* who faithfully served the church in Cenchrea, a port city not far from Corinth. Phoebe is the first female *deacon* mentioned in the Bible.

Recap

- Think of Romans as *the* textbook of the Christian faith. In it, Paul answers the most frequently asked faith questions. It is a must read for Christians.

- Remember that when Paul wrote this letter he had never been to Rome. For this reason, he tried his best to thoroughly explain salvation and the Christian life to his readers.

- To understand Romans, it is very important to become familiar with the vocabulary. Take time to learn the meanings of the new terms.

Read it!

- Read Romans now. At a casual reading pace, it will take you 50 minutes. Read it in one sitting or in two 25-minute sessions.

Self-study / Group discussion questions

- Why did Paul write this letter to the Christians in Rome? What was he trying to accomplish? What do you think his objectives were?

- In your own words, what does it mean to be *completely saved*? What part of your life needs to be *saved* the most?

- How is the formation of a new Christian group like sowing seeds in fertile soil? What can we learn from this vivid visual image?

Insights that we can apply today

There is no condemnation for those who belong to Christ Jesus.

—Romans 8:1

Like it or not, because all humans are sinful by nature, you and I are guilty of offending God and must someday stand before him to face the consequences. That is, of course, unless someone takes our place, which is exactly what Jesus did on the cross. And when you acknowledge that Jesus died for you, God declares you "not guilty." Now there is no longer any need for you to feel shameful or fearful before God.

Intro to 1 Corinthians

On Tuesday, October 29, 1991, swirling high above the North Atlantic a few hundred miles off the coast of Nova Scotia, three massive weather systems were poised to collide one into another with deadly force. The first one, a low-pressure system that had formed over mid-America was now spinning like a cyclone and intensifying off Newfoundland's Grand Banks.

The second, a huge arctic air mass powered by the jet stream, had moved rapidly down a southeastern trajectory on a collision course with the *low* as it passed over New England and headed out to sea. When the frigid Canadian air crashed into the warm air of the *low*, a storm of ferocious intensity was born: a very nasty Nor'easter.

Meanwhile, just to the south, a tropical hurricane named Grace, a storm hundreds of miles across and packing sustained winds of 100 miles per hour had just left Bermuda and was heading rapidly northwards.

Within hours, Grace slammed headlong into the other two creating a monster storm that weather professionals would call "the storm of the century," the **perfect storm**. Its 100-foot waves were among the highest on record. Its devastating winds and tides pounded the Eastern Atlantic Seaboard for days, wreaking havoc from Nova Scotia to North Carolina.

In AD 53, swirling high above Corinth, a Greek mega-city strategically located on a narrow strip of land that separated two seas, a different kind of storm was brewing; a unique kind of atmospheric disturbance was occurring. And though not blown by winds, this Corinthian storm would prove to be every bit as explosive as the Halloween storm of 1991.

As Paul walked southwest along the dusty 40-mile Roman road that joined Athens to Corinth, spiritual forces of evil were gathering at the fortress rock Acrocorinth, high above the city, making final preparations for the violent confrontation that was about to occur. The surpassing power of the gospel of Christ, embodied in a hunched-over, five-foot-five Jewish tent maker was about to collide with Satan's most sinful city.

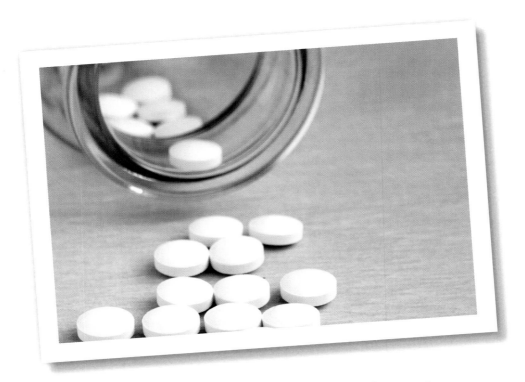

1 Corinthians' theme:
Eleven migraines

1 Corinthians

Writer	Paul
Date written	AD 57
Place written	Ephesus—3rd journey
Recipients	Church in Corinth
Theme	Eleven migraines

> I appeal to you, dear brothers and sisters... Let there be no divisions in the church. —1 Corinthians 1:10

A short review of New Testament history may go a long way to help us understand how in the world *eleven migraines* has anything to do with the theme of this second of Paul's letters to churches. So here goes.

On his third missionary journey, shortly after arriving in Corinth, Paul met Aquila and Priscilla, a kindly Jewish couple from Rome. Since they also made tents for a living, he joined up with them in their enterprise. Through Paul's faithful witness, both soon came to faith in Christ and returned the favor, joining up with him in *his* enterprise, the work of establishing God's kingdom in Corinth.

Paul and his new-found partners faced two stiff challenges as they began to evangelize the city. The first was rampant and unchecked immorality. "The famous commercial prosperity of the first Corinth soon returned," says Bible scholar Donald Guthrie, "and so did its notorious reputation for sexual license, which had spawned a new word, to 'Corinthianze.'" The city's name became a verb: to Corinthianize meant to practice sex with abandon.

The second challenge was the arrogance of the local intellectuals. Though Corinth was not academically on par with Athens (the philosophy capital of the world), it was said that no one could walk along any street in Corinth without encountering "a sage" (philosopher). At best, converted intellectuals were difficult to work with. At worst, they were unbending, arrogant radicals.

"In such an atmosphere of moral laxity and intellectual pride," continued Guthrie, "the Corinthian church was bound to be troubled with many problems arising from the impact of Christianity on its pagan environment." As Paul wrote this letter, 11 of these problems had turned critical (pass the Excedrin).

Why this letter was written

During the 18 months that Paul had faithfully taught the word of God in Corinth, a thriving church had emerged, in spite of the negative cultural influences that had threatened its existence. But, as all good things must come to an end, Paul needed to move on. So, boarding a ship with Aquila and Priscilla, he sailed to Ephesus.

After dropping his partners off in town, Paul continued his journey to Caesarea in Palestine and then home to Antioch where he remained for about a year. Then, feeling the itch to get back on the road, Paul headed out again, bound for Ephesus, where he was reunited with Aquila and Priscilla. Paul would stay there for three years.

Meanwhile, some 220 sea miles due west across the Aegean, things in the church in Corinth were coming unglued. In recent months, without Paul's strong and active leadership in church affairs, small issues had developed into big ones, to a point where the church was starting to tear apart at the seams.

"The Church in Corinth was the most brilliant crown of his labor," says Frederic Godet, the famous Swiss theologian, "but it was also that which he had the greatest difficulty in defending against the inroads of moral evil and the attacks of his adversaries."

One day, while Paul was at work in Ephesus, a woman named Chloe came to see him. She and her family had recently visited the church in Corinth and had returned with some very troubling news. Among church members, said Chloe, said Chloe, strong competing factions have formed, shattering the oneness of the believers. Church meetings have deteriorated into shouting matches. "I'm of Paul," one group would yell. "I'm of Apollos," another would respond. Paul, begged Chloe, you've *got* to do something.

As if that wasn't trouble enough, a three-man delegation from Corinth soon showed up at Paul's door carrying a letter from their church. The letter contained a laundry list of problems that they desperately needed Paul to address.

In all, 11 major issues faced Paul as he sat down to compose this letter. He organized them into five categories and began to tackle them head-on, one by one.

A brief outline of the letter

Since unity was the most urgent issue facing the church, Paul addressed it first and dealt with it fully (four chapters). Then he proceeded to hit moral issues (next critical), followed by instructions on proper worship.

Near the end of the letter, Paul wrote extensively about Christian resurrection. Then, he wrapped up his correspondence with practical teaching on Christian finances—how we all should set aside part of our resources to support those who are in need.

	Chapters
Oneness—no divisions should exist within a church	1-4
Moral issues—incest, lawsuits, sin, marriage, idols	5-10
Worship issues—women's role, spiritual gifts, communion	11-14
Resurrection—the longest discussion in the Bible	15
Giving—how to systematically give money	16

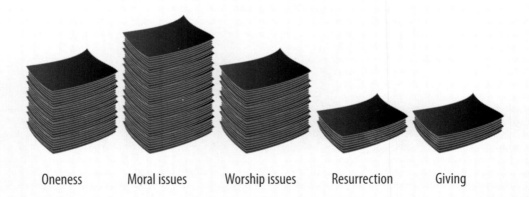

Oneness   Moral issues   Worship issues   Resurrection   Giving

Paul's eleven migraines and where to find them

Of all the churches that Paul had established across Europe and Asia Minor, Corinth was by far the most challenging. "The church at Corinth was a vexing problem to him because of its instability," says Merrill Tenney, world-renowned Bible teacher and former dean of Wheaton College. "Since it was largely composed of Gentiles who had no training in the Old Testament Scriptures, and whose religious and moral antecedents were the exact opposite of Christian principle, much teaching was required to bring them up to the place of spiritual maturity."

Here they are:

1. Factions, parties, divisiveness. **1 Corinthians 1:1—4:21**

2. A church scandal: incest. **5:1-8**

3. Lawsuits: Christians suing each other. **6:1-11**

4. General immorality. **5:9-13; 6:12-20**

5. Marriage issues. **7:1-40**

6. Eating meat sacrificed to idols. **8:1-11:1**

7. Women's roles in worship. **11:2-16**

8. Worship behavioral issues. **11:17-34**

9. The best way to use spiritual gifts. **12:1-14:40**

10. Christian teaching on resurrection. **15:1-58**

11. Christian giving. **16:1-9**

How to navigate 1 Corinthians

1. **Understand what Paul is doing**

    The content of 1 Corinthians may seem scattered to you when you read this letter. That's because it is. Remember that Paul is addressing a number of issues and answering many questions, one by one.

2. **Realize that not everything applies to us today**

    When you try to apply the teachings of this letter to yourself, realize that in some cases, Paul is correcting problems that had arisen in the context of the Corinthian culture of his day. Today, we don't have to worry about whether we should purchase surplus meat that had earlier been offered to idols, or whether women should cover their heads in public. We can, however, learn a lot by watching how Paul deals with these issues.

3. **Look for Christ and His cross**

    As you read, notice how Paul directs the believers to Christ and to his cross as the unique solution to all of their issues (1 Cor 1:18, 2:2, etc.).

Unique things about 1 Corinthians

1st Corinthians is actually 2nd Corinthians (say what?)

In 1 Corinthians 5:9, Paul refers to an earlier letter that he had sent to the Corinthians. This former letter was not preserved for our use, possibly because it may have been of a local and entirely circumstantial nature. Some Bible scholars believe that Paul had carried on an active ongoing correspondence with the members of the church in Corinth during the years that he was apart from them. Only two of these letters remain.

There are six *now* sections

Starting with chapter seven, the text is divided into six *now* sections. Paul opens each section with the Greek word for *now* to let his readers know that he is moving on to the next topic. Here are the *nows*: 7:1, 8:1, 11:2, 12:1, 15:1 and 16:1.

1 Corinthians has the *love* chapter

One of the most frequently quoted chapters in the entire Bible is 1 Corinthians 13, commonly known as the *love chapter*. This beautiful chapter on the superiority, nature and character of love is read extensively at weddings and has been included in the Church of England's *Book of Common Prayers.*

Paul made tents for a living

Paul's occupation was tent making. As with Peter, Paul's job choice would prove to be prophetic. Just as Jesus asked Peter, the fisherman, to become a "fisher of men," Paul, the tent maker, redirected his skills to build the church, the "house of God." In Acts 18:1, Paul rushed out of Athens and hurried to get to Corinth. But why? Most likely, it was because he wanted to arrive before the start of the regional "Olympic Games" to make lots of tents to sell to the tens of thousands of visiting spectators who would soon arrive and completely overwhelm local accommodations.

Recap

- When you think of 1 Corinthians, picture a hurricane making landfall. This is like the gospel of Christ crashing into the most sinful city in the world.

- Think of the 11 issues of the Corinthian church as Paul's 11 migraines, piled one on top of another.

- Visualize Corinth's problems in five groups: oneness, moral issues, worship issues, doctrine and giving.

Read it!

- Read 1 Corinthians now. At a casual reading pace, it will take you 50 minutes. Read it in one sitting or in two 25-minute sessions.

Self-study / Group discussion questions

- What was it about the Corinthian society at Paul's time that made it so challenging to establish a church there? Can you think of any places that might present similar challenges today?

- The theme, *Eleven migraines* speaks to the 11 serious issues that had reached a boiling point in the church in Corinth. How did Paul address these issues? What would you have done if you were Paul? How would you have reacted?

- The first issue that Paul addressed in this letter was the problem of disunity among the Corinthian believers. Why is maintaining unity within a church so important? What might happen if the oneness among the members is lost?

Insights that we can apply today

No eye has seen, no ear has heard, and no mind has imagined what God has prepared for those who love him.   —1 Corinthians 2:9

In this verse, Paul describes the incredible state of blessedness Christians can participate in, both in this life, and in the next one. Today, God's Spirit brings joy, peace, love and strength as gifts to those who love Him. Have you experienced these things? If not, you can. And if you already have, "you ain't seen nothin' yet."

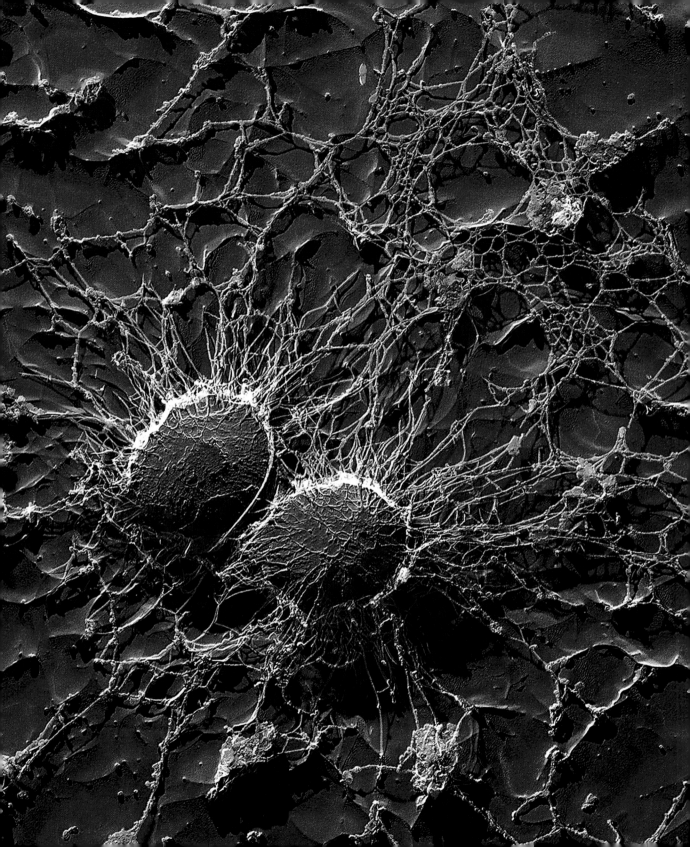

Intro to 2 Corinthians

OXFORD, ENGLAND, 1941—At a local hospital, Arthur Jones, a 15-year-old boy, undergoes hip surgery and begins to recover. But suddenly he spikes a nasty fever, probably caused by a Staph infection on his newly-inserted metal hip pin (opposite, magnified 50,000 times), and his wound becomes septic.

Though doctors administer Sulfa drugs, his body fails to respond. His fever persists for two weeks. Most likely, Arthur *will* die. In 1941, eighty percent of patients who pick up post-surgery infections do.

Dr. Howard Florey, head of the School of Pathology at Oxford University, decides to try a radical procedure. He infuses the boy with an experimental antibiotic that, though successfully tested on lab mice, had been tried on only one other human being, who eventually died. Miraculously, within two days, Arthur's fever breaks, and he fully recovers. The penicillin worked.

Welcome to the perfect metaphor for 2 Corinthians.

Paul's earlier surgical letters to Corinth, though life saving, had offended a few of the believers. Subsequently, as their emotional wounds fester, the church, the body of Christ, becomes particularly vulnerable to outside attacks. Soon **bad germs**, in the form of false apostles, find entrance into the body through the disgruntled members and attach themselves to their newfound hosts.

Once safely inside, the intruders quickly disarm the community's natural immune systems with eloquent and persuasive words. They then release powerful toxins—thoughts about *another Jesus*—into the believers' minds. As their lying persists, the saints become stupefied—they can't easily discern truth from fiction. Soon, the body's normal functions begin to break down. The organs stop working. The heart starts to fail. The patient is dying.

Wasting no time, Dr. Paul grabs pen and paper and injects a mega dose of spiritual antibiotic into the Corinthian church. "We (spiritual doctors) don't wage war as humans do," writes Paul. "We use God's mighty weapons, not worldly weapons, to knock down the strongholds (germs)… We will punish everyone (the microbes) who remains disobedient" (2 Corinthians 10:4-5).

As the Corinthians read this, their fever breaks. The Paulicillin worked.

2 Corinthians' theme:

Hit me with your best shot

2 Corinthians

Writer   Paul
Date written   AD 58
Place written   Greece—3rd journey
Recipients   Church in Corinth
Theme   Hit me with your best shot

> I don't consider myself inferior in any way to these "super apostles."
>
> —2 Corinthians 11:5

Paul's staunch defense of God's truth and of the ministry that Christ had entrusted to him emerges as *the* dominant theme of this three-part letter. As he hears from afar the harassing voices of the small group of opponents huddled within the Corinthian church, Paul stands up, looks the bad guys square in the eyes and challenges them to a fight. Mano a mano.

"Hit me with your best shot," he says, rather confrontationally.

There are at least two ways to interpret Paul's daring challenge. The first is to say, "Is that *all* you've got?" By this time in Paul's spiritual career, he had seen it all. In his travels across Palestine, Asia Minor and Europe to evangelize the world for Christ, he had been threatened, beaten, whipped, shipwrecked, drowned, frozen, starved, chained, imprisoned, caned, stoned and dumped on the side of a road and left for dead.

That his Corinthian foes were sticking out their tongues and calling him names—you coward, you fraud, you stuttering preacher—was laughable. Sticks and stones might break Paul's bones, but names could *never* hurt him.

A second way to interpret our theme would be to say, "My dad is bigger than your dad." God was clearly in Paul's corner. His ministry bore God's stamp of approval. When he spoke, Christ spoke. He stood firmly on the side of the truth and had an arsenal of spiritual weapons. And who do we have in the opposite corner of the ring? A ragtag bunch of apostle wannabies cobbled together by the devil. Need we say more?

Why this letter was written

When the dust finally settled, Paul wrote at least four letters to the church in Corinth and visited them at least three times. To better understand why Paul wrote 2 Corinthians, scholars have attempted to reconstruct the circumstances which preceded its writing, as follows:

Paul's 1st visit. Paul visits Corinth for the first time during his second missionary journey. There he establishes a church and remains in town for 18 months, teaching the new believers and caring for them. He then says goodbye for now, sails to Ephesus and returns home to Antioch via Jerusalem. This story can be found in Acts 18.

Paul's 1st letter. Fast forward two years. Paul is again visiting Ephesus. He decides to write a letter to the church in Corinth to remind them not to associate with people who claim to be Christians yet practice sexual sin. Scholars will later refer to this as *the previous letter*. Paul mentions it in 1 Corinthians 5:9-11. This first letter is not preserved and is not in the Bible.

Paul's 2nd letter. The Corinthians receive Paul's first letter but do not interpret it correctly. Other questions arise. The church's leaders write a letter to Paul outlining their concerns. A three-man delegation hand-carries this letter to Ephesus. Paul reads it and responds back with his second letter to them, known today as **1 Corinthians**.

Paul's 2nd visit. Sometime later, Paul gets wind of other issues swirling around Corinth and decides to pay the church a visit. For some unknown reason, the trip turns out to be a disaster and he is forced to beat a hasty retreat to Ephesus. Paul mentions this trip in 2 Corinthians 2:1. Bible scholars will later nickname this second trip *his painful visit*.

Paul's 3rd letter. After returning to Ephesus, Paul writes a third letter to the Corinthians, known as his *sorrowful letter*, in response to his painful visit to Corinth. The letter is quite severe and corrective and is written "in great anguish, with a troubled heart" (2 Cor 2:3-4). It will be painful for the Corinthians to read (2 Cor 7:8-9). This letter is not preserved and is not in the Bible.

Paul's 4th letter. Meanwhile, things aren't going well for Paul in Ephesus (poor guy). Christianity is getting a bad name, and he is being blamed. A riot breaks out and he is forced to leave town (this always happens). He heads northwest towards Macedonia, and along the way meets up with his friend and co-worker Titus who has just returned from a trip to Corinth.

Titus has good news and bad news. First, the good news: a majority of the Corinthian believers have responded well to Paul's *sorrowful letter*. They support his ministry and sincerely appreciate his loving care for them.

Now the bad news: there is a mutiny in progress. A vocal minority, consisting of self-appointed *super apostles*, is in full revolt against Paul. These evil people are trying their best to overthrow his position of influence and to undermine his credibility.

Paul is both relieved and concerned at the same time as he sits down and writes his fourth Corinthian letter (**2 Corinthians**). In it, he both expresses his gratitude to his faithful followers for their ongoing support and blasts his enemies with the truth. Near the end of the letter, Paul announces that he is on his way to see them (again): "This is the third time I am coming to visit you" (2 Cor 13:1).

Paul's 3rd visit. Paul and Titus continue their travels through Macedonia. Within six months, they arrive in Corinth. They spend three months there. Paul's letters have been effective. Conditions have improved dramatically.

A brief outline of the letter

The framework of 2 Corinthians has four parts, two larger chunks and two smaller ones. The Finances piece in the middle contains the most extensive discussion of the principles of Christian giving in the New Testament.

	Chapters
Ministry—this is what I preach and teach	1-5
Reconciliation—be reconciled to God and to us	6-7
Finances—join in on the fund-raising for needy churches	8-9
Strong medicine—hit me with your best shot, you rebels	10-13

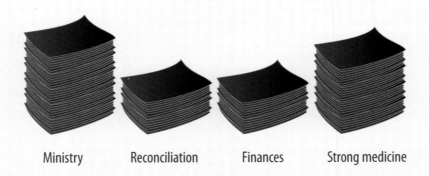

Ministry   Reconciliation   Finances   Strong medicine

Verses that illustrate Paul's unshakable confidence in God

In the midst of his tumultuous dealings with the Corinthian church, and in spite of his own sufferings, Paul remains steadfast in his trust in God and his confidence in God's power to bring him through his trials.

But thank God! He… continues to lead us along in Christ's triumphal procession. **2 Corinthians 2:14**

Since God in his mercy has given us this new way, we never give up. **4:1**

We are pressed on every side by troubles, but we are not crushed. **4:8**

We are perplexed, but not driven to despair. **4:8**

We are hunted down, but never abandoned by God. **4:9**

We get knocked down, but are not destroyed… That is why we never give up. **4:9,16**

Though our bodies are dying, our spirits are being renewed every day. **4:16**

We don't look at the troubles we can see now… we fix our gaze on things that cannot be seen. **4:18**

We are always confident… For we live by believing and not by seeing. **5:6-7**

I don't consider myself inferior in any way to these "super apostles." **11:5**

As the truth of Christ is in me…no one will ever stop me from boasting about this. **11:10**

I will give you all the proof you want that Christ speaks through me. **13:3**

How to navigate 2 Corinthians

1. **Look for Paul's personality**

    Paul unveils his heart more in 2 Corinthians than in any of his other writings. His rich personality shines through every page. According to Bible scholar Merrill Tenney, "The human Paul is very much in evidence: his feelings, desires, dislikes, ambitions and obligations are all spread before his readers." Look for these.

2. **Realize that Paul has been forced to defend himself**

    For years, Paul lived humbly in service to his Lord and Savior Jesus Christ. Now, for the purpose of knocking out his opponents, he is forced to brag about himself. This is very uncomfortable and difficult for him to do. Yet, he uses the word *boasting* at least 13 times. Notice this awkwardness.

3. **Know where you are**

    Keep the three sections of the letter in mind as you read. Remember that Paul is seeking to accomplish three completely different tasks with one letter. First, in chapters 1-7, he is providing encouragement to his supportive majority. Second, in chapters 10-13, he is defending himself against the mutinous minority. And in between, he is providing instructions about fund-raising for needy churches in other locations (chapters 8-9).

Unique things about 2 Corinthians

Did you know...

Paul itemizes his sufferings for others' benefit

Paul defends himself as an apostle of the church in Corinth by listing the kinds of sufferings he has endured in his years of following Christ. Included in the list are beatings, whippings, stonings, imprisonments, shipwrecks, insomnia, hunger, nakedness and freezing cold, to name a few. The complete list is found in 2 Corinthians 11:22-33.

Paul took a secret trip to heaven

To shut the mouths of those who were trying to undermine his credibility, Paul tells a story of his secret roundtrip to "the third heaven." Apparently, for God's own private reasons, Paul was escorted there and heard and saw amazing things. Paul wasn't quite sure whether he was having an out-of-body experience or not, but he *was* certain that it happened. You can read all about it in 2 Corinthians 12:2-4. By including this story in his letter, he was saying to his critics, "Top this one."

Paul had a thorn in the flesh

Following Paul's visit to heaven, to keep him from becoming proud, God allowed him to suffer some sort of debilitating medical condition, which he called, "a thorn in my flesh." Based on clues found in other parts of the New Testament, Bible teachers have speculated that this infirmity may have been severe headaches, malaria, epilepsy, or opthalmia, an eye disease. For more, read 2 Corinthians 12:7 and Galatians 4:13-15.

Recap

- When you think of 2 Corinthians, picture a hospital with the Corinthian church as the patient and Paul as the doctor.

- Picture Paul standing up against his opponents to defend himself. Hear him say, "Hit me with your best shot."

- Remember that there are three sections to the letter—encouragement, finances and strong medicine.

Read it!

- Read 2 Corinthians now. At a casual reading pace, it will take you 30 minutes. Read it in one sitting or in two 15-minute sessions.

Self-study / Group discussion questions

- Why do Christ-followers need to be on guard against false teachings? Why is it vitally important to know the truth revealed in the Bible?

- What does the theme of this letter, "Hit me with your best shot," tell us about Paul? What does it tell us about his love for the church?

- Does it surprise you that Paul had so much back and forth correspondence and traffic with the church in Corinth? Why or why not?

Insights that we can apply today

We ourselves are like fragile clay jars containing this great treasure.

—2 Corinthians 4:7

The Christian life is a partnership. And a paradox. We partner with Christ when we make ourselves available to him for God's kingdom work. Yet, he provides the power as he carries out his work through us. Thus, the paradox. We are often weak. But he is strong. We are fragile. He is solid. We are flaky. He is always there. This is the way it is. And it's wonderful!

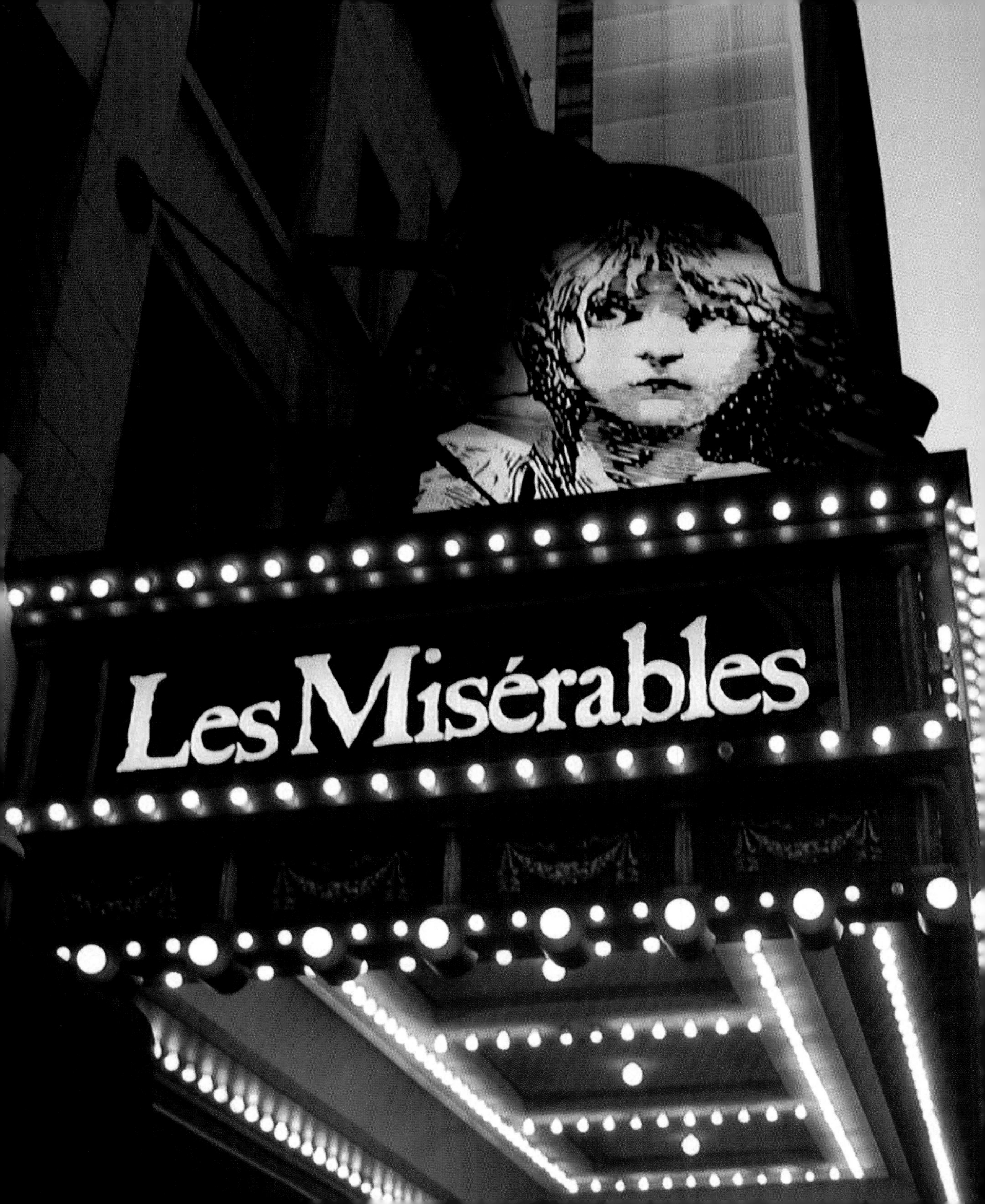
Les Misérables

Intro to Galatians

In the late 1700s, life in France for the teeming peasant class was awful. Enslaved to a hardscrabble existence under rigid laws and heavy taxation to support the extravagant lifestyles of the privileged few, these miserable ones, *"Les Misérables,"* teetered on the brink of starvation.

That is, until July 14, 1789.

On that particular Tuesday morning, a large mob of armed and angry commoners, who had had quite enough of King Louis XVI's aristocratic reign, stormed a prison in Paris (the Bastille) shouting, "**liberté, égalité, fraternité.**"

And voilà, the French Revolution had begun.

Within weeks, the National Assembly of France, the new representatives of the French people, had drafted its Declaration of Rights—a document that espoused the principles of the Revolution and embodied the first two elements of its three-part battle cry:

Liberty—that men are born free and are to remain free. Law can only prohibit such actions as are hurtful to society. No group or individual can exercise authority (over others) that doesn't proceed directly from the nation.

Equality—that men are born equal in rights. Social distinctions may be founded only upon the general good.

A third element—**brotherhood**—came from the cause itself; the idea that French people were standing together, unified in support of common ideals—in this case, the restoration of human rights to all French citizens.

Some 1,734 years earlier, in a small corner of eastern Turkey, the world had heard a similar battle cry. This time the trumpeter was the Apostle Paul himself, who loudly proclaimed "**liberté, égalité, fraternité**" for all Christians across Galatia, especially those who were being lured into religious slavery by slick-talking Jewish fundamentalists.

"Christ has truly **set us free**," shouted Paul. "Now make sure that you stay free...There is no longer Jew or Gentile, slave or free," cried Paul. "For **you are all one** in Christ Jesus...dear **brothers and sisters**."

Welcome to Galatians—the Bible's French Revolution.

Galatians' theme:

Run hard from bad religion

Galatians

Writer	Paul
Date written	AD 55
Place written	Ephesus
Recipients	Churches in Galatia
Theme	Run hard from bad religion

I am shocked that you are turning away so soon from God.

—Galatians 1:6

If you lived on the planet during Old Testament times, you could have a blessed, God-pleasing life by loving God with all your heart and by keeping his commandments. By doing these two things, your inner desires and your outward behaviors would line up with God's will for you.

Back in those days, Old Testament laws like the Ten Commandments functioned like guardrails on a highway, installed for your safety. They kept you on the straight and narrow so you could enjoy the life that God intended for you as you motored through your days. And they also kept you from flying off a cliff, so to speak, badly hurting both yourself and others.

But, when Jesus came, everything changed. Through his death and resurrection, he opened the way for everyone on earth to have a personal relationship with God Himself. By receiving Christ, his Spirit could live in our hearts and direct our lives Godward from the inside out.

And with Jesus in the driver's seat, we no longer need the guardrails. He is more than able to keep us humming right along. In this scenario, once having handed Jesus the keys and fastened our seat belts, it would be stupid (and insulting to our driver) for us to ignore him and listen instead to kibitzers who insist that we install new guardrails before starting our car.

But, that's exactly what happened to the Galatian believers at Paul's time. Though they had already become Christians by their faith in Christ, Jewish legalists insisted that they must obey Old Testament laws too. This was a bad thing for this reason: as the believers paid increasing attention to outward religious practices, they drifted farther away from God Himself (as evidenced in the verse above). Paul's advice: That's bad religion. Run away—and fast.

A brief outline of the letter

Galatians divides itself nicely into three bite-sized pieces. Paul first presents his credentials to his readers so that they will pay attention to what he says. Then, he reads them their rights. And finally, he directs them to stay away from the bad guys and to live free in Christ (nicely done).

	Chapters
Champion of freedom—Paul's qualifications	1-2
Declaration of freedom—Christ sets us free from law-keeping	3-4
Life of freedom—live your life in this freedom	5-6

Champion   Declaration   Life

Verses that highlight our liberté, égalité, fraternité

These verses give voice to Paul's battle cry for freedom, equality and brotherhood. Notice how forcefully and urgently he makes his points.

I am shocked that you are turning away so soon from God. **Galatians 1:6**

If anyone preaches any other Good News… let that person be cursed. **1:9**

Some so-called Christians—false ones, really…sneaked in to spy on us and take away our freedom. **2:4**

Oh, foolish Galatians! Who has cast an evil spell on you? **3:1**

How foolish can you be?… Why are you now trying to become perfect by your own human effort? **3:3**

Christ has rescued us from the curse pronounced by the law. **3:13**

God sent him (his Son) to buy freedom for us… so that he could adopt us. **4:5**

Now you are no longer a slave but God's own child. **4:7**

So Christ has truly set us free. Now make sure that you stay free. **5:1**

You have fallen away from God's grace. **5:4**

You were running the race so well. Who has held you back…? **5:7**

But don't use your freedom to satisfy your sinful nature. **5:13**

How to navigate Galatians

1. ## Realize that Paul is fighting against religious fanatics

   The tone of Galatians is confrontational and rightfully so. False Christians have sneaked into the churches to trap the believers with legalities and trip up their faith. Paul, their spiritual father, is protective of his little lambs and warns them that trouble is brewing.

2. ## Pay attention to faith

   Faith is topic number one in Galatians. In this brief six-chapter letter, Paul mentions *faith* 21 times. As you read this letter, watch how he uses this word. Paul preaches faith in Christ to us. We, in turn, are justified by faith, receive righteousness by faith, live by faith and are children of God by faith living in the household of faith. Faith has come.

3. ## Pay attention to law

   If faith is topic number one, the law is topic number two. You will run into the word *law* 31 times in this letter, most often in a negative context. The law refers to the laws God gave the Hebrew people through Moses and other regulations that were added later. The *works of the law* are religious practices people take part in to try to please God. Through Christ, these have been replaced by the new laws of Spirit, life and love.

Unique things about Galatians

Did you know...

Galatia was a region, not a city

Each of the first nine of Paul's New Testament letters was written to a specific church in a specific city except one—Galatians. This letter was written to many churches, groups of believers who lived in cities across Galatia, a Roman province located in what's known today as eastern Turkey.

Paul had more than 1,001 Arabian nights

Shortly after Paul became a Christian, he left civilization behind and took off for the Arabian Desert. He lived there for three years, receiving revelations and one-on-one training from Christ Himself. Just as Jesus' original 12 disciples got three years of training from their Master, Paul did too (perfect).

Galatians is a declaration of freedom

Many Christian teachers think of Galatians as the Emancipation Proclamation of Christian liberty. In January 1863, Abraham Lincoln proclaimed freedom for the slaves of the Confederacy. No longer would their physical lives be under the control and direction of others. In Galatians, the Apostle Paul proclaimed freedom for all Christians. No longer would their spiritual lives be under the control of other people's religious laws.

No time to say goodbye, hello...

All of Paul's letters open with long greetings and thanksgivings except one—Galatians. Here, Paul is as impatient as the White Rabbit in Alice in Wonderland as he jumps immediately into the subject of his letter. "I am shocked that you are turning away so soon from God" (Galatians 1:6).

Recap

- Liberté, égalité, fraternité. Remember that Galatians is the French Revolution of the New Testament.

- Think of Galatians as the Emancipation Proclamation of Christian freedom.

- Living by Old Testament law was once the way to go. Now that Christ has come, the law is no longer necessary. We follow him instead.

Read it!

- Read Galatians now. At a casual reading pace, it will take you 16 minutes.

Self-study / Group discussion questions

- Freedom, equality, brotherhood are the three watchwords for Christians in Galatians. Which one of these three words impresses you the most? Is one more important than another? Have you experienced all three?

- Do you find yourself living more by outward behaviors or by God's inner leading? What can you do to change the mix?

- Faith in Christ is the bedrock of Christianity. In your own words, what is the difference between believing in Christ and doing religious works?

Insights that we can apply today

The Holy Spirit produces this kind of fruit… love, joy, peace, patience, kindness, goodness, faithfulness… —Galatians 5:23

How can you tell whether a peach tree is healthy or not? Look at its fruit. How can you tell whether your spiritual life is healthy or not? Look at *your* fruit. In these two verses, Paul lists nine human virtues, produced by the Spirit and manifested in our lives if our relationship with God is tight and vibrant. How healthy is your spiritual life? Which of these virtues would you like to experience more?

Intro to Ephesians

No trip to Paris is complete without a visit to the Louvre, one of the world's most prestigious museums. And no visit to the Louvre is complete without having adequate face time with the museum's three great resident ladies, the Venus de Milo, Nike (Winged Victory of Samothrace), and of course, Mona Lisa, one of the most famous art objects in the history of the world.

Our third lady, captured in Leonardo Da Vinci's pint-sized masterpiece, resides comfortably in her own newly refurbished gallery in the Denon wing of the museum's first floor. There, she graciously receives six million smiling visitors a year, all of them eager to see whether she'll smile back at them.

Mona Lisa, better known to sixteenth century Italians as Monna (Mrs.) Lisa Gherardini, was the wife of Francesco del Giocondo, a successful cloth merchant from Florence. Though Leonardo painted her portrait 500 years ago, she lives on today as one of his greatest artistic achievements.

Many art lovers consider the **Mona Lisa** Da Vinci's *piéce de rèsistance* because of the painting's creative brilliance and enduring critical acclaim. According to biographer Giorgio Vasari, artists at Da Vinci's time, wowed by the painting's life-like imagery, flocked to see it. Says Vasari, "This work is executed in a manner well calculated to astonish all who behold her."

"Today's art critics call attention to the painting's mystery and harmony," says Louvre Curator Jean-Pierre Cuzin. "But the first art historians to describe it emphasized its striking realism, pointing out 'the lips that smile' and 'the eyes that shine.'" The painting has a character entirely its own.

In like manner, many Bible lovers believe that Paul's letter to the Ephesians is *his* Mona Lisa, a masterpiece of Christian thought, executed in a manner well-calculated to astonish all who read it. In no other biblical letter can we both sound the depths of God's infinite mysteries (chapters 1-3) and benefit from Paul's practical, down to earth advice (chapters 4-6) at the same time.

"Among the Epistles bearing the name of St. Paul," says Scottish Bible teacher S.D.F. Salmond, "there is none greater than this, nor any with a character more entirely its own... In the judgment of many who are entitled to deliver an opinion, it is the grandest of all Pauline letters."

Ephesians' theme:
Masterpiece!

Ephesians

Writer	Paul
Date written	AD 63
Place written	Rome—during Paul's 1st imprisonment
Recipients	Church in Ephesus and other churches
Theme	Masterpiece!

For we are God's masterpiece. —Ephesians 2:10

At the end of the book of Acts, Paul is living in Rome in a rented apartment. He is being held there under house arrest, waiting for a hearing before Caesar for a crime he didn't commit. He will stay there for two years.

What might seem to some as negative circumstances turn out to be quite positive for him, for now he has plenty of time to rest, to think, to have conversations with Jesus—and to write four letters, Colossians, Philemon, Ephesians and Philippians.

The first pair of these so called *prison epistles* is written to resolve issues that have arisen among Christians in one location, Colossae, an ancient city located in today's Turkey. As Paul completes these two writings, a faithful courier named Tychicus stands by, ready to hand-carry them to their intended recipients 1,000 miles away (it will be a long walk).

Before Tychicus can finish lacing up his sandals (and pack his lunch), Paul grabs his arm. "Wait a second," he says. "Since you'll be traveling through Asia Minor anyway, there's another letter that I need you to deliver."

With that, Paul walks over to his desk, sits down and begins to write Ephesians. This one will be a *circular letter* destined first for believers in Ephesus and from there circulated to Christian groups in other places.

In it, Paul warmly welcomes the Ephesians into God's glorious family by showing them spectacular things God has done for them. Since there are no issues for Paul to deal with, his writing is free to soar. And soar it does:

"He raised us from the dead along with Christ and seated us with him in the heavenly realms… God can point to us in all future ages as examples… of his grace and kindness toward us… we are his masterpiece."

A brief outline of the letter

Paul writes Ephesians in two parts. Each has three chapters. In the first part, he displays the heavenly, spiritual truths that Christians should understand and experience. In the second, he lays out practical advice to help our daily living. In the first, Paul focuses on beliefs and, in the second, on behaviors. The two parts perfectly harmonize with each other.

	Chapters
Beliefs—heavenly visions, compelling sights	1-3
Behaviors—earthly practices, sound advice	4-6

Beliefs   Behaviors

Verses that show the process of God's masterpiece

Paul describes the steps God takes to create his masterpiece: how he gathers spiritually dead people from all walks of life, enlivens them by his Spirit and weaves them together with Christ into the fabric of his spiritual dwelling place on earth. This beautiful tapestry of God-redeemed humanity is his best work, which he eagerly displays for the entire universe to see (marvelous).

God has now revealed to us his mysterious plan regarding Christ. **Ephesians 1:9**

You used to live in sin, just like the rest of the world, obeying the devil. **2:2**

But God is so rich in mercy, and loved us so much, that… he gave life to us. **2:4**

For he raised us from the dead along with Christ and seated us with him in the heavenly realms. **2:6**

So God can point to us in all future ages as examples of the incredible wealth of his grace and kindness. **2:7**

For we are God's masterpiece. He has created us anew in Christ Jesus. **2:10**

Don't forget that you Gentiles used to be outsiders. **2:11**

In those days you lived apart from Christ. **2:12**

You lived in this world without God, without hope. **2:12**

But now you have been brought near to him through the blood of Christ. **2:13**

You… are no longer strangers and foreigners. …You are members of God's family. **2:19**

We are carefully joined together in him, becoming a holy temple for the Lord. **2:21**

How to navigate Ephesians

1. **Notice how Paul describes divine revelations**

   At some time in Paul's Christian life, God revealed to him the mystery of his will, the plan of his eternal purpose. Paul describes these divine insights, which had been hidden from mankind for generations, in vivid detail in chapters 1-3. Read slowly. Don't miss them.

2. **Watch for Paul's word pictures of the church**

   In this letter, Paul creates metaphors to illustrate four aspects of the church. In Ephesians 2:21-22, the church is believers built together into a temple for God's residence; in 4:4, it is Christ's body, expressing him, and through whom he can move and work; in 4:24, it is likened to God's *new man*, a brand-new spiritual entity, and in 5:25-32, it is the bride of Christ, whom he loves, for whom he gave his life and to whom he is devoted forever.

3. **Pay attention to oneness**

   Unity is an overarching theme of Ephesians. Paul says that God has created one band of believers out of two groups, Jews and non-Jews, people who once hated each other. This amazing, now-unified assembly testifies of God's transforming work in members' lives. The new group guards a seven-fold oneness—one Body, one Spirit, one hope, one Lord, one faith, one baptism, one God—with the Spirit's help. Lots of *ones* (Ephesians 4:3-6).

Unique things about Ephesians

Did you know. . .

The church in Ephesians is universal, not local

In Paul's other New Testament letters, the word *church* means a group of Christian believers meeting together in a specific location. However, in Ephesians, it has a different meaning. Here, the church is universal in scope. It includes all believers from all places throughout all time. We exist together, whether in heaven or on earth, and in spirit constitute God's one family.

Christians are God's Masterpiece

The Greek word *poiema*, (*masterpiece* or *workmanship* in most English Bibles), is used twice in the New Testament. The first time is in Romans 1:20 where Paul likens the universe—God's outstanding *physical* creation—to the handiwork of an expert craftsman. The second time is here in Ephesians 2:10 in reference to the church—God's incredible *spiritual* creation (nice).

Ephesians and Colossians are twins

If we laid Ephesians and Colossians side by side, we would discover that 78 of the 155 verses in Ephesians are identical (or nearly so) to verses in Colossians. This should not surprise us since at the time Paul wrote this letter, he had just finished writing Colossians— its lofty ideas still occupied his thoughts.

We have God's armor

In Ephesians 6:10-18, Paul asks his readers to stand strong in their faith. Then he vividly describes the spiritual armor they should slap on as they go out into the world to do battle with the devil. This protective gear includes five defensive pieces—breastplate, belt, shoes, shield and helmet—and one offensive weapon—the sword of the Spirit.

Recap

- Ephesians is Paul's masterpiece. The church is God's masterpiece.

- God has created one beautiful tapestry of redeemed humanity from scattered, spiritually-dead people from all walks of life.

- Ephesians is written in two parts. In the first we see heavenly visions to help our beliefs. In the second we find life lessons to help our behaviors.

Read it!

- Read Ephesians now. At a casual reading pace, it will take you 16 minutes.

Self-study / Group discussion questions

- Think about the universal church—a composition of believers throughout all time and space. Paul calls this spiritual entity *God's masterpiece*. What makes this church so special, mind-boggling and spectacular?

- How is a masterpiece created? Does an artist know his work will be his masterpiece before he begins? Or does it just happen? Did God intentionally create his masterpiece, or did it just happen?

- Why is maintaining Christian unity so critically important to God and to us? What happens when Christians divide themselves from each other because of issues, practices or strongly held beliefs? Who benefits?

Insights that we can apply today

**So now you Gentiles are no longer strangers and foreigners…
you are members of God's family.** —Ephesians 2:19

One of Paul's purposes in writing this letter was to welcome all believers into God's one, big, happy family. Before becoming Christians we are strangers, to each other and to the faith, living isolated lives outside of God's plan and provision. Now, through faith, we are reborn as God's children and are introduced to hundreds, if not thousands of brothers and sisters. Welcome to God's family. Make yourself at home.

Intro to Philippians

JUNE 6, 1944, 4:15 AM—With storms over the English Channel forecast to dissipate, **General Dwight D. Eisenhower**, Supreme Commander of the Allied Forces in Europe, gives the go-ahead to launch Operation Overlord.

"You are about to embark upon a great crusade," Eisenhower tells his men. "You will bring about the elimination of Nazi tyranny over the oppressed peoples of Europe and security for ourselves in a free world." With these few words, 5,000 ships, 13,000 aircraft and 160,000 troops start to move.

D-day has finally arrived. Within 24 hours, Allied soldiers reach the coasts of Normandy and with great difficulty establish a beachhead. In ten weeks, they liberate France and, within a year, force Germany to unconditionally surrender. France and England celebrate. People are dancing in the streets.

As an expression of thanks from a grateful nation, French President Charles De Gaulle sends Eisenhower a message, letting him know that he will be receiving France's most prestigious award, the Order of the Liberation.

Eisenhower, flattered by this lofty honor, responds to de Gaulle with a thank-you note of his own: "I am deeply grateful for your fine message and for the wonderful honor which you have bestowed on me... With assurance of my continued regard and admiration, Dwight D. Eisenhower."

In Acts 16, the Bible records a similar invasion, slightly smaller in scale yet equally important. Paul, Silas, Timothy and Luke are about to embark on a great crusade to bring about the elimination of spiritual tyranny over the oppressed peoples of Europe and provide for their eternal security.

Their first stop is Philippi. Through Paul's preaching, a number of local residents are liberated from their sins, and a church is born. People are dancing in the streets. As an expression of thanks from a grateful flock, the new believers, though poor, financially support Paul's ministry—for years.

Some ten years later, during the time that Paul is in prison in Rome, a messenger from Philippi arrives with yet another financial gift. Paul, flattered by this lofty honor, responds with a grateful acknowledgement. He begins, "I thank my God upon every remembrance of you... making request for you all with joy."

Welcome to Philippians—Paul's thank-you note.

Philippians' theme:
Joy, joy, joy

Philippians

Writer	Paul
Date written	AD 63
Place written	Rome—during Paul's 1st imprisonment
Recipients	Church in Philippi
Theme	Joy, joy, joy

Always be full of joy in the Lord. I say it again—rejoice.

—Philippians 4:4

Paul's letter to the Philippians is unique among his New Testament writings. There are no crises for him to mediate. There are no serious issues for him to resolve. There are neither deep teachings nor lofty revelations for him to pass along to his readers.

Rather, the letter is a joy-fest, each page exuding more joy than the last. In Rome, Paul rejoices in the Lord in spite of his chains. In Philippi, the church members rejoice in the Lord in spite of their sufferings. And each party rejoices all the more when it hears that the other party is rejoicing.

Like giddy newlyweds on their honeymoon, joy is sloshing out all over the place. Face it—Paul and the Philippians are crazy in love. It's obvious. Of all the churches Paul has planted, the church in Philippi is hands down his favorite. She is the apple of his eye. But why?

Some say it's because Philippi is the first church Paul founded in Europe— a significant accomplishment, a meaningful milestone for him. Others think it's because the Philippians are such a generous and loving people, who with hearts the size of Texas demonstrate their fierce loyalty to Paul by rallying to support him financially.

Others suggest it's because the church had remained issue-free, sheltered from outside religious attacks that had plagued other Christian congregations. For whatever reason, the fact is that Paul and this particular group of spiritual children share an especially close, loving relationship.

The result is blatant, unabashed, unmitigated happiness.

In short—joy, joy, joy.

A brief outline of the letter

Philippians can also be thought of as a letter written by a traveling father to his loving children back home. He has recently received a surprise gift from them and eagerly sends his reply. To ease their minds, he first opens a conversation about how he's doing. Then, he thinks of them and suggests a few practical things they should take care of in the household. Next, he reminds them to keep things moving forward during his absence. And finally, he thanks them for being his joy and sends them his love.

	Chapters
News—things are going fine with me in Rome	1
Homework—keep your oneness, serve humbly	2
Goal—keep going, press on, gain Christ	3
Joy—Rejoice in the Lord always!	4

| News | Homework | Goal | Joy |

Verses that rejoice

Paul expresses joy, gladness and rejoicing more in this short letter than in all of his other writings combined. Here are some examples:

> *Whenever I pray, I make my requests for all of you with joy.* **Philippians 1:4**

> *So I rejoice. And I will continue to rejoice.* **1:18**

> *I will remain alive… to help all of you…experience the joy of your faith.* **1:25**

> *Make me truly happy by agreeing wholeheartedly with each other.* **2:2**

> *But I will rejoice even if I lose my life.* **2:17**

> *I want all of you to share that joy.* **2:17**

> *Yes, you should rejoice, and I will share your joy.* **2:18**

> *Welcome him with Christian love and with great joy.* **2:29**

> *Whatever happens, my dear brothers and sisters, rejoice in the Lord.* **3:1**

> *Dear friends… you are my joy and the crown I receive for my work.* **4:1**

> *Always be full of joy in the Lord. I say it again—rejoice.* **4:4**

> *May the grace of the Lord Jesus Christ be with your spirit.* **4:23**

How to navigate Philippians

1. **Meet two Philippians**

    Read the story of Paul's first visit to Philippi in Acts 16:11-40. Shortly after Paul's team arrives in town, two characters appear on stage. The first is Lydia, a businesswoman who sells purple fabrics. She is Paul's first European convert. The second is a Roman jailor, brought to faith following an earthquake. Both, in turn, bring their family members to faith.

2. **Pay attention to** *you* **and** *me*

    Philippians is by far the most informal and intimate of Paul's letters. His writing style is easy and comfortable, and he uses personal pronouns a lot. Here's an exercise: take out a pen and as you read this short letter start to finish, count how many times Paul says, *I* and *me* (hint: more than 100). He also says *you* and *yours* over 70 times. This is intimacy.

3. **Study the "Christ Hymn"**

    A critical section of this letter is Philippians 2:5-11, known as the "Christ Hymn" since it was written in poetic form. Here, in one of the earliest statements of the Christian faith, Paul makes crystal clear: 1) that Christ is God, 2) that he humbled himself, became a man and died to save us from our sins and 3) that he is now reigning over everything as Lord of all.

4. **Read Paul's autobiography**

    In Philippians 3:2-15, Paul lists his impressive accomplishments and credentials. Then, he says that all of these former things are rubbish compared to his new life's work: serving Christ and getting to know him.

Unique things about Philippians

Did you know. . .

Caesar's bodyguards and household heard the Gospel

During his first imprisonment in Rome, Paul was under the constant care of Caesar's Imperial Guard, crack troops who took turns guarding him by handcuffing him to themselves. Imagine what fun Paul had talking about Jesus to these guys, one at a time. Talk about a captive audience. Over time, they all heard the Good News. Paul says that during this time, a large number of people from Caesar's household became Christians (Philippians 1:12-14).

Paul preached for free

Paul wasn't a paid preacher. He received no regular wages from any of the many local churches he had founded. Rather, he worked as a tent-maker to provide for his own needs. At times, however, he did honor the Philippians' love for him by graciously receiving and acknowledging their financial support.

Two feuding ladies

Women of substance played prominent roles in the church in Philippi. In this letter, Paul calls our attention to two of them. Unfortunately, these lovely ladies are feuding. And their names, Euodia and Syntyche, sound strangely symbolic. The first: *you odious*—she's bent out of shape about something. And the other: *soon touchy*. Need we say more? (Philippians 4:2)

Don't worry, be happy

Paul reveals two secrets of true happiness and passes them along to the Philippians. One is that worrying about things doesn't help. What *does* help is to tell God what you're worried about, sharing your concerns with him. Another is that in whatever circumstances you find yourself, whether in riches or poverty, you can find contentment in Christ.

Recap

- Philippians is Paul's casual and intimate thank-you note.

- He and the church in Philippi have a joyful thing going. He is their doting father, and they are his loving children.

- The letter is like correspondence from a traveling dad: here's what's happening with me, I love you and I look forward to seeing you soon.

Read it!

- Read Philippians now. At a casual reading pace, it will take you 12 minutes.

Self-study / Group discussion questions

- Philippians is about thankfulness. How do you express your thanks to other people? What makes saying "Thank you," so powerful to both parties? What can we do to become more thankful people?

- Is joy a part of your daily experience? If not, why not? How can we live more buoyant, joyful lives?

- Paul suggests that we can be freed from anxiety by inviting God to join us in our circumstances. Is this a common practice among people you know? If not, why not?

Insights that we can apply today

Forgetting the past. . . I press on to reach the end of the race and receive the heavenly prize.   —Philippians 3:13-14

The Christian life is a marathon—a long race towards the goal of being all that we can be for God and of experiencing all that he has for us. As with running, we do best when we keep our eyes focused straight ahead on Christ and our thoughts in the present. Agonizing over the past is a waste of time. We learn from our experiences and move on. Happy running.

Intro to Colossians

If you asked Bible teachers to close their eyes and think of something that reminds them of Colossians, the **Empire State Building** might immediately come to mind. This magnificent building—massive, unshakable, solidly grounded on the earth, yet lofty and preeminent—is the perfect image of Christ as portrayed in this fabulous letter. Both stand in the solitude of themselves.

Built in 1931, America's most admired building, an icon of strength and transcendence, reigned supreme as earth's tallest man-made structure for over 40 years. How it won first place is another story.

And as is the case with many things, you can blame it on the French. They started it way back in 1889 when architect Gustave Eiffel threw down the gauntlet. In that year, his 984-foot tower, built to commemorate the 100th anniversary of the French Revolution, stole the title of "world's tallest" from our own beloved Washington Monument.

As you might expect, this did not sit well with architects, engineers and capitalists on this side of the Atlantic, who at the turn of the century jumped en masse into the tall-building-construction contest. In New York City in the early 1900s, skyscrapers started popping up all over the place. But by 1924, the Woolworth Building, Manhattan's tallest at 792 feet, was still a good 200 feet short of Eiffel's mark.

That's when two architects, William Van Alen and Craig Severance, entered the fray with rival projects. When the construction dust settled in the spring of 1930, Van Alen's project, the Chrysler Building (at 1,045 feet), was named world champion, a title it would retain for only a short time. For one year later, a building 1,250 feet tall and named after the Empire State opened its doors. The rest is history.

In the past 80 years, over 110 million people have visited the Empire State Building's 102nd floor observation deck. The view from the top is breathtaking. But whatever you do, don't look down. Instead, take Paul's high-altitude advice and look up. "Set your sights on the realities of heaven… not the things of earth" (Colossians 3:1-2).

Colossians' theme:
Summa Christo!

Colossians

Writer	Paul
Date written	AD 63
Place written	Rome—during Paul's 1st imprisonment
Recipients	Church in Colossae
Theme	Summa Christo!

He is first in everything. —Colossians 1:18

Epaphras is a friend of Paul's and a leader in the church in Colossae. He has just traveled 1,000 miles from this small city located in western Turkey to visit Paul in prison in Rome. Sorry to say, this is not a social call. Epaphras has a big problem and he desperately needs Paul's advice.

"There are a number of phony teachers," explains Epaphras, "who have started to infiltrate our church. They are pawning off a strange brew of philosophy, religious practices and magic as the way to get to heaven. This stuff is beginning to confuse the daylights out of the believers. Something has to be done. But what?"

Paul thinks for a minute—then, feeling God's presence, he picks up his pen and begins to write this letter. When he's done, he hands it to Tychicus, his faithful courier, and asks him to hand carry it back to Colossae and read it out loud to the church.

"Here you go. Lord willing, this should do the trick," says Paul.

In the letter, Paul uses strong language to build logical arguments to counteract the poisonous ideas the false teachers are spreading. He reasons that since Christ is God's Son, he is the highest, strongest and most capable Person in the universe, reigning high above any man-made ideas or religious rites. In two Latin words, he is Summa Christo, the exalted one, God's Summa cum Laude, highly honored, transcendent over all. This preeminent Christ is fully sufficient to meet all of our needs, including transporting us to heaven

"Since the believers have a direct, personal relationship with such a Christ," says Paul, "why in the world would they settle for such empty, shallow stuff? They just need to realize what they already have in Christ."

A brief outline of the letter

The structure of Colossians is identical to the structure of Ephesians. In both letters, Paul opens with statements of truth for Christians to embrace, followed by advice on how to live our lives now that we've embraced them.

	Chapters
Beliefs—Christ is supreme and rules over everything	1-2
Behaviors—avoid the bad guys, look up towards Christ	3-4

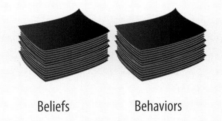

Beliefs   Behaviors

Verses that show Christ's preeminence

In Colossians, Paul has a lot to say about Christ's superiority. In point after point, Paul demonstrates Christ's greatness and warns the Colossian believers not to settle for anything less.

Christ is the visible image of the invisible God. **Colossians 1:15**

Through him God created everything in the heavenly realms and on earth. **1:16**

He existed before anything else, and he holds all creation together. **1:17**

He is first in everything. **1:18**

God in his fullness was pleased to live in Christ. **1:19**

In him lie hidden all the treasures of wisdom and knowledge. **2:3**

I am telling you this so no one will deceive you with well-crafted arguments. **2:4**

Don't let anyone capture you with empty philosophies and high-sounding nonsense. **2:8**

In Christ lives all the fullness of God in a human body. **2:9**

You are complete through your union with Christ. **2:10**

Since you have been raised to new life with Christ, set your sights on the realities of heaven. **3:1**

Let the message about Christ, in all its richness, fill your lives. **3:16**

How to navigate Colossians

1. **Understand the strange brew**

   The particular strain of heresy that threatened the Colossian believers was a blend of false, man-made teachings pulled from three non-Christian belief systems: Greek philosophy, Jewish legalism and Oriental mysticism. As you read Colossians, watch how Paul argues against the following falsehoods:

   Here are the lies:

   > Jesus is not God. **Colossians 1:15**
   >
   > God did not create the earth. **1:16**
   >
   > Jesus is only one of many angelic beings. **1:16-17**
   >
   > Higher knowledge (philosophy) is the way to find God. **2:8**
   >
   > Jewish circumcision is required for salvation. **2:11-14**
   >
   > Christians must keep Jewish dietary laws and holy days. **2:16-17**
   >
   > Christians must worship angels. **2:18**

2. **Study Christ**

   Colossians contains the highest "theology" of Christ in the New Testament. In this letter, Paul explains three things: 1) who Christ is, 2) what he has accomplished and 3) what he's done for his followers. Take out a sheet of paper, make three columns, and as you read, list as many of these three things as you can.

3. **Consider God's three mysteries**

   In Colossians, Paul presents three mysteries, deep truths that were hidden from mankind for ages, but that God revealed to his believers at Paul's time. Be on the lookout for them and think about each one. Here they are:

   > The mystery of Christ living in us. How is this possible? **1:26-27**
   >
   > The mystery of God: Christ. How did God become a man? **2:2**
   >
   > The mystery of Christ. How mysterious is God's plan of salvation? **2:3**

Unique things about Colossians

Did you know…

Colossians and Philemon are siblings

Paul's letters to the Colossians and Philemon are like siblings. They have a lot in common. They were written at the same time, at the same place (Rome) and were co-authored by Timothy. They were both addressed to Christians in the same city, Colossae, and were hand-delivered, at the same time, by the same person, Tychicus, accompanied by his same sidekick, Onesimus. And in both, Paul sent greetings from the same people, namely, Epaphras, Aristarchus, Mark, Luke and Demas.

Christ *spoils* his foes

After the Greeks won a battle, they walked through the battlefield and stripped their fallen enemies of all their clothing and armor. These spoils of war were then attached to tall wooden poles (called *trophies* in Greek) and paraded into town, amidst singing and cheering, in victory festivals. This scene is vividly captured in Colossians 2:15, where Christ, victorious in his resurrection, has disarmed and spoiled his spiritual enemies and marches triumphantly with his trophies, making a public spectacle of them.

Mark reconciles with Paul

In Acts 13:13, at the beginning of Paul and Barnabas' first missionary journey, Mark, their young apprentice, completely fails Paul by bailing out on the team and heading for home. Now some 18 years later, in the closing paragraph of Colossians, we find Mark reunited with Paul, standing by his side in Rome. Somewhere along the way, Mark, apparently, had apologized.

Recap

- Christ in Colossians is like the Empire State Building. Beautiful, lofty and preeminent. He is Summa Christo!

- The false teachings that threaten the faith of the Colossian believers are a strange brew of religious, philosophical and magical ideas.

- Paul fights against these heresies by using strong language and sound, logical arguments.

Read it!

- Read Colossians now. At a casual reading pace, it will take you 11 minutes.

Self-study / Group discussion questions

- Paul's purpose in writing his letter to the Colossians was to clearly present the truth about Christ and refute the false teachings about him. Why is it critically important for Christians to clearly understand the truth about Christ? What can happen to us if we don't?

- In **Colossians 3:15-20**, Paul presents many facts about who Christ is and what he has done. Which of these impresses you the most? Why?

- In **Colossians 3:15-17**, Paul gives us three words of advice: 1) let the peace of God rule in your hearts, 2) let the word of Christ dwell in you richly and 3) whatever you do, do it in the name of the Lord Jesus. How do you actually do these things? What do these practices look like for you?

Insights that we can apply today

Work willingly... as though you were working for the Lord rather than for people. —Colossians 3:23

The Christian life is a life of enjoyable service. And just like servants who serve at the pleasure of the king, or Cabinet members who serve at the pleasure of the President, Christians serve at the pleasure of the Lord. This is a great attitude to maintain in everything we do, whether it's working at our jobs, helping our communities, raising children or washing the car. We have the privilege of serving the living God. Think about it...

Intro to 1 & 2 Thessalonians

In both of these short letters, Paul praises the Thessalonian Christians for their superhuman faith in the face of intense anti-Christian persecution. Yet, unusually heroic behavior was not uncommon to the Greeks.

At Thermopylae, along a coastal road a few hours north of Athens, stands an imposing statue of **Leonidas**, warrior King of Sparta, a city-state of ancient Greece. This striking image marks the spot where, in 480 BC, Leonidas, 300 Spartans and a few thousand other Greeks miraculously held hundreds of thousands of invading Persian soldiers at bay—for three days.

During the first two days of the battle, through fierce hand-to-hand combat, the Greeks successfully repelled their invaders' assaults, helped to a great extent by a very narrow mountain pass that severely restricted the enemy's progress. But by daybreak on day three things had turned ugly, for during the night the Persians had found a way around the pass. This meant that it was only a matter of time before the Greeks would be outflanked, surrounded and crushed.

Leonidas called his men together, told them that the situation was hopeless and urged them to retreat while they still had time. But, as for him and the 300 Spartans, they would stay to the bitter end and die fighting. While many of the soldiers left, about a thousand joined Leonidas.

As the Persians closed in, they ordered the Greeks to surrender their weapons. Leonidas fired back, "Come and take them," to which the Persians responded, "If each of our soldiers shoots one arrow into the air, a dark cloud will form over your heads that will blot out the sun." A Spartan named Dienices replied, "So much the better. We will fight in the shade."

Within three hours, all of the Greeks lay dead. But by delaying the Persians, they had accomplished a higher purpose, for during the three-day standoff, the entire population of Athens had been evacuated to safety. Leonidas had saved the Greek culture, which 100 years later would rule the world, creating the perfect environment for the coming of Jesus Christ to the planet. And for Paul to establish a brave church in Thessalonica.

1 Thessalonians' theme:
Jesus is coming back soon

1 Thessalonians

Writer	Paul
Date written	AD 53
Place written	Corinth
Recipients	Church in Thessalonica
Theme	Jesus is coming back soon

The day of the Lord's return will come unexpectedly...

—1 Thessalonians 5:2

Paul's second missionary journey had brought him, for the first time, to Europe. When his ship docked at the port city of Neapolis, Greece, he headed inland to Philippi with his traveling companions, Luke, Silas and Timothy. They remained in Philippi for some time preaching and teaching.

From Philippi, they traveled west to Thessalonica, a major metropolitan city, where, through Paul's speaking in the synagogue, some Jews and a large number of devout Greeks became Christians. For three weeks, Paul taught these new converts the basics of the Christian faith and, while he was at it, told them about the second coming of Christ.

Unfortunately, Paul was forced to leave town quite abruptly when a band of irate Jews hired thugs to hunt him down and kill him. As he was being smuggled out of town by local friends under the cover of darkness, he became concerned for the welfare of the new disciples he had left behind.

So, when he reached Athens, Paul sent Timothy back to Thessalonica to see what was going on. The good news was that the Thessalonian believers were standing strong (thank you very much), in spite of intense waves of religious persecution that battered them.

The bad news was that some of the faithful had developed wrong and worrisome ideas about what happens to believers who die before Jesus comes back. They feared that their deceased Christian loved ones would be left behind when Christ returns to rescue his followers. This upset them very much.

Sensing their concern, Paul sent this letter to them to clear up the misunderstanding—no, the Christians who have passed away will not be left behind—and to encourage the believers to hang in there.

A brief outline of the letter

This letter can be studied in two parts. In the first three chapters, Paul encourages and inspires his readers by retelling the story of his three-week visit to Thessalonica. Then in chapters 4-5, he corrects their mistaken ideas about Christ's second coming and tweaks a few of their more blatant behavioral issues (such as laziness).

	Chapters
Encouragements—hang in there, stand firm	1-3
Corrections—the dead believers will be okay	4-5

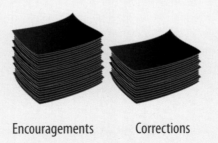

Encouragements   Corrections

Verses that highlight Christ's return

In 1 Thessalonians, Paul has much to say about Christ's second coming, more than in any other New Testament letter. Here are some of the places where he mentions Jesus' return.

You are looking forward to the coming of God's Son from heaven. **1 Thessalonians 1:10**

He is the one who has rescued us from the terrors of the coming judgment. **1:10**

What will be our proud reward… as we stand before our Lord Jesus when he returns? **2:19**

You stand before God our Father when our Lord Jesus comes again. **3:13**

When Jesus returns, God will bring back with him the believers who have died. **4:14**

We who are still living when the Lord returns will not meet him ahead of those who have died. **4:15**

For the Lord himself will come down from heaven with a commanding shout. **4:16**

We who are still alive… will be caught up in the clouds to meet the Lord in the air. **4:17**

Now concerning how and when all this will happen… we don't really need to write you. **5:1**

The day of the Lord's return will come unexpectedly, like a thief in the night. **5:2**

You won't be surprised when the day of the Lord comes like a thief. **5:4**

May your whole spirit and soul and body be kept blameless until our Lord Jesus comes again. **5:23**

How to navigate 1 Thessalonians

1. **Visualize the context**

    Luke tells the story of Paul's first visit to Thessalonica in Acts 17:1-15. As you read this account, visualize religious extremists running around town, yelling, screaming and creating turmoil for the new Christians. Put yourself in the believers' sandals. How would you react if you were there?

2. **Notice Paul's encouraging words**

    1 Thessalonians is like a letter of encouragement to soldiers on the front lines of a battlefield. Paul writes to acknowledge the believers' bravery in a spiritual fight in the face of overwhelming odds. As you read the letter, notice how Paul goes out of his way to praise their valiant stand.

3. **Watch for Christ's coming**

    As you read 1 Thessalonians, watch for details about Christ's second coming. Look for these as you would signposts along a highway. Study their context carefully. You'll be surprised how much new information is provided there.

4. **Pay attention to people behaving badly**

    In most of his letters, Paul opens with words of thanksgiving, continues with a section on Christian teaching and ends with practical helps. This letter is no exception. In chapters four and five, Paul asks his readers to address a few of their more serious behavioral issues. Laziness is one. Sexual freedom is another. There are more. Try to identify them.

Unique things about 1 Thessalonians

Did you know...

Christians will be abducted

According to 1 Thessalonians 4:13-18, in the end times, when Christ returns and God judges the evil on the planet, Christian believers who are alive will be snatched out of harm's way by Jesus himself, God's heavenly "thief" (how exciting can it get?). How and when this so-called *rapture* will happen is open to debate. But the result will be the same—Christ's people will be with him forever.

This church had a rather dramatic birth

The church in Thessalonica was born into an environment of severe anti-Christian persecution. Yet, because of the unusually powerful presence of God's Spirit among them, the young congregation not only survived, they thrived. So much so, that news of their heroic stand for Christ spread throughout the region. They became Paul's boast among the churches.

Mind your own business

Sorry to say, a few of the Thessalonian believers were work-challenged. For whatever reason, they were just plain lazy—and rather than work, they preferred to burn up countless hours spreading gossip. Because of this, Paul tells them to "mind your own business and work with your hands."

A string of glittering diamonds

In 1 Thessalonians 5:16-22, Paul ties together a dozen short, pithy sayings: godly pieces of advice designed to help raise the believers' spiritual and social lives to higher ground. Bible teacher S.W. Green likens this beautiful series of short encouragements to "a string of glittering diamonds."

Recap

- When you think of Thessalonians, think of Leonidas and his Spartans as they courageously defended what they believed in and deeply loved.

- When you think of Thessalonians, think of Christ returning to earth.

- Remember that 1 Thessalonians has two sections: an encouragement section (chapters 1-3) and a corrections section (chapters 4-5).

Read it!

- Read 1 Thessalonians now. At a casual reading pace, it will take you 10 minutes.

Self-study / Group discussion questions

- In your own words, explain why Paul wrote this letter. Why did he structure it the way he did? Why did he think that the letter would help the situation?

- Paul had founded the church in Thessalonica. Based on his fatherly care for the believers, he urged them to change a few bad behaviors. If you were there, listening to the reading of this letter, would you have responded positively to Paul's advice? Why or why not?

- What has this letter taught you about Christ's second coming? What more would you want to know? Why?

Insights that we can apply today

Always be joyful. Never stop praying. Be thankful in all circumstances, for this is God's will for you. —1 Thessalonians 5:16-18

These days, joy is like an endangered species. It's getting harder and harder to find. Yet, unlike many other folks on the planet, Christians are, by and large, a joyful lot, often in spite of downright awful circumstances. This is because day by day, they choose to stay attached to Christ, the Joy Giver. How much joy are you experiencing these days? Not much? Have you been in touch with the Joy Giver recently? If not, you can be. Have a conversation with him—that's what prayer is all about. Then, give thanks for the many blessings God has given you. And see what happens.

2 Thessalonians' theme:
But not THAT soon

2 Thessalonians

Writer	Paul
Date written	AD 53
Place written	Corinth
Recipients	Church in Thessalonica
Theme	But not THAT soon

> Now, dear brothers and sisters, let us clarify some things about the coming of our Lord Jesus Christ.   —2 Thessalonians 2:1-2

A short time after sending his first letter to the Thessalonians, Paul heard the news that the church was thriving, in spite of severe persecution. It also seemed that the clarifications Paul had provided in his letter had resolved the believers' misconceptions about the Lord's second coming.

However, a new issue had now developed. With false prophecies and forged letters, agitators from outside the church had created a high level of anxiety inside the church by convincing some of the believers that the end of the world had come.

As a result, rumors were flying all over the place, suggesting that Jesus was on his way back to earth. This alarming news led some of the believers to quit their jobs to watch for his imminent return—or at least that's what they said. Sounds like it was time for Paul to make a few more corrections.

And that's just what he did, writing this second letter to assure the Thessalonians that the world was not ending quite yet and to give them two landmark events to watch for which would signal Christ's coming.

"Don't be fooled by what they say," said Paul. "For that day will not come until: 1) there is a great rebellion against God and 2) the man of lawlessness is revealed." This man is Antichrist, mentioned here by Paul for the first time in the New Testament. He will be an evil superman, appearing on earth at the end of time to oppose Christ and claim that he is God.

"Don't you remember that I told you about all this when I was with you?" concluded Paul, assuring one and all that Christ is not coming back THAT soon. He then ordered everyone to go back to work if they ever wanted to eat food again.

A brief outline of the letter

The structure of Paul's second letter is similar to the structure of his first. Both lead with encouragements and end with corrections. In this case, there is more correcting than encouraging.

	Chapters
Encouragements—hang in there, stand firm	1
Corrections—Christ is NOT coming yet—so get back to work	2-3

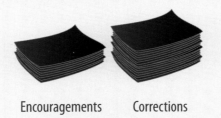

Encouragements   Corrections

Verses that highlight Christ's second coming

In this letter, Paul speaks about the second coming of Christ in the context of continuing persecution and false reports that were circulating. His advice to the faithful is to stay away from rumor-mongers and to hang tough. Here are a few key verses that mention these things:

God will provide rest for you who are being persecuted. **2 Thessalonians 1:7**

And also for us when the Lord Jesus appears from heaven. **1:7**

When he comes on that day, he will receive glory from his holy people. **1:10**

Let us clarify some things about the coming of our Lord Jesus Christ. **2:1**

Don't be...alarmed by those who say that the day of the Lord has already come. **2:2**

That day will not come until there is a great rebellion against God. **2:3**

And the man of lawlessness is revealed—the one who brings destruction. **2:3**

With all these things in mind… keep a strong grip on the teaching. **2:15**

The Lord is faithful; he will strengthen you and guard you from the evil one. **3:3**

Stay away from all believers who live idle lives. **3:6**

"Those unwilling to work will not get to eat." **3:10**

As for the rest of you… never get tired of doing good. **3:13**

How to navigate 2 Thessalonians

1. **Study Antichrist**

    In 2 Thessalonians 2:1-13, Paul provides details about Antichrist—who he is and what he will do when he arrives on the scene. Read this portion carefully, word by word, and as you do, make a list of these details. It is also helpful to study these verses in two or three different Bible translations.

2. **Notice Paul's encouraging words (again)**

    The persecution that the believers were suffering at the time when Paul wrote his first letter had intensified. Notice as you read this letter that Paul is doing his best (again) to praise them for their heroic stand for Christ and to encourage them, by God's grace, to keep it up.

3. **Watch for Christ's coming (again)**

    In this short letter, Paul provides new information about Christ's return. Look for it. Most of it deals with the actions Christ will take when he returns to earth, including how he will punish those who cause the believers' suffering and how he will annihilate Antichrist (good riddance).

4. **Pay attention to people behaving badly (again)**

    Some of the inappropriate conduct that Paul called out in his first letter had become more pronounced among some of the local Christians. Paul once again draws our attention to two issues in particular, laziness and gossip. As you read, look for these, and see how many more issues you can find.

Unique things about 2 Thessalonians

Did you know...

Someone sent forged letters

One of the tactics the local belligerents used to scare the Christians and throw them off balance was to forge Paul's signature on phony letters and circulate them among the faithful. Paul refers to one of these fake letters in particular that claimed that the end of the world had already arrived (2 Thess 2:2). For this reason, Paul authenticates his writing with his own signature (2 Thess 3:17).

Paul, Timothy and Silvanus are role models

To counteract the inappropriate influences of a few Christians who were behaving badly, Paul asks people to "withdraw" from these folks and puts Timothy, Silvanus and himself forward as hard-working role models for the believers to imitate.

There are no Old Testament quotes (at all)

According to Acts, the church in Thessalonica consisted of "some" Jews and a "great many" local Greeks. For this reason, neither of Paul's two Thessalonian letters contains any quotes from the Old Testament. None. The Greeks in the congregation would not be familiar with them.

No work, no eat

A few of the lazier believers took advantage of the excitement that was caused by talk of the Lord's return by refusing to work and by sponging meals from other people. In chapter three, like a good father, Paul lays down the law and puts these freeloaders on notice: "Anyone not willing to work should not eat."

Recap

- When you think of 2 Thessalonians, think of Christians who are suffering persecution for their faith. And think of Paul encouraging them.

- When you think of 2 Thessalonians, remember that Christ is coming back soon—but not THAT soon.

- Remember that 2 Thessalonians has two sections: an encouragement section (chapter 1) and a corrections section (chapters 2-3).

Read it!

- Read 2 Thessalonians now. At a casual reading pace, it will take you 6 minutes.

Self-study / Group discussion questions

- If you were Paul, how would you go about providing encouragement to the Thessalonian believers? What would you say or do?

- Does Paul do an adequate job of describing Antichrist and his activities? Why doesn't he provide more details? Should he? Why or why not?

- Jesus is coming back to earth someday. Knowing this, how should Christ-followers live? What should we do differently?

Insights that we can apply today

Never get tired of doing good.—2 Thessalonians 3:13

When it came to taking care of human needs, Jesus set the gold standard, both in his teachings and his actions. He not only taught about feeding the poor, healing the sick and freeing the oppressed, he did it tirelessly—all day, everyday. At times, taking care of other people's needs can be quite overwhelming, can't it? Hang in there—and be strengthened by God. By the power of his Spirit, we can keep on making a difference in the lives of the people around us.

Paul's Letters to People

Intro to 1 Timothy

1 Timothy is a letter from a veteran coach (Paul) to his star student-athlete (Timothy) during half-time of the most challenging *game* of Timothy's life. It's been very tough going for Timothy so far. His opponents have been a handful. Their trash talking has smothered his self-confidence. He's losing faith—and fast. It's time for a pep talk from Paul. Welcome to 1 Timothy. Enjoy reading the inspiring words of the Bible's legendary coach.

Speaking of legendary coaches, let me introduce you to another one. His name is **John Wooden**. John was the most successful sports coach who ever lived. Himself a three-time All-American basketball player at Purdue, Wooden coached the UCLA men's basketball team for 27 years and led the Bruins to 10 NCAA championship titles, including seven in a row.

Four times his teams had undefeated seasons, with 30 or more wins. His home record at UCLA's Pauley Pavilion was 149 wins and 2 losses. During one stretch, the Bruins won 88 consecutive games.

For years, other coaches have tried to discover the secrets of Coach Wooden's success. Some believe it was the way he treated his players—that he loved them like his own children. "I never had a player I didn't love," said Coach Wooden. "Love is the most powerful four-letter word."

Others have said that it was the tireless work ethic he forged into his players. "There is no substitute for hard work," taught the coach. "If we are going to become all that we are capable of becoming, we need to work hard. But we also need to be intentional about the hard work."

A few have wondered out loud if Coach Wooden's phenomenal success might just have something to do with his love for certain books. "Drink deep from good books," he reminded his players, "especially the Bible" (hmm… the Bible?). Could it be that the "Wizard of Westwood" mined some of his maxims from Paul's letters? Consider the following from 1 Timothy:

"I, Paul… am an apostle of Christ Jesus… Timothy… you are a true son in the faith… love is the purpose of my command… don't fail to use the gift the Holy Spirit gave you… keep on doing those things. Give them your complete attention… Never give up."

1 Timothy's theme:
Hold on, I'm coming

1 Timothy

Writer   Paul
Date written   AD 65
Place written   Macedonia, Greece
Recipient   Timothy
Theme   Hold on, I'm coming

> I am writing these things to you now, even though I hope to be with you soon...   —1 Timothy 3:14

Though the Bible doesn't say so, it seems probable that after waiting in Rome for two years for his case to come to trial, Paul finally has his day in court. And by the end of the proceedings, he is acquitted of the charges brought against him and is released. Since he had already spent two years in prison in Caesarea (Palestine) before coming to Rome, this is the first time in four years that Paul is a free man.

Joined by Timothy, his young co-worker, Paul leaves Rome and travels to Asia Minor, among other places, to revisit and strengthen some of the churches he had established earlier. The church in Ephesus is one of them.

During their stay in this large city, Paul is called away to Macedonia for some emergency. Not wanting to interrupt their local work, Paul leaves Timothy in charge, gives him a few verbal instructions and heads out.

As time passes, fearing that he might be detained longer than expected, Paul writes this letter to highlight the urgent issues Timothy should address in his absence and to strongly encourage him.

Timothy's first order of business is to confront the local loud-mouthed *experts* who are teaching the believers irrelevant stuff that contradicts Christian truth. "These windbags," says Paul, "ramble on endlessly. And they don't have a clue what they're talking about."

Paul also asks Timothy to sort out local church-leadership problems and reminds him to watch his behavior, since he is supposed to be a role model for the believers to emulate. Realizing that Timothy is young, timid and most likely overwhelmed, Paul closes the letter by strongly challenging him to fight against his natural desire to quit, urging him to "hang in there" until he gets back.

A brief outline of the letter

In this first of two letters to Timothy, Paul lays out an interim plan for Timothy to follow while leading the church during his extended absence. The structure of the letter visually looks like a triangle. It has three parts: a short introductory portion, a long middle section and a short ending.

	Chapters
Teachers—shut the false teachers' mouths	1
Instructions—how to lead the church while I'm away	2-5
Hold on—fight the good fight	6

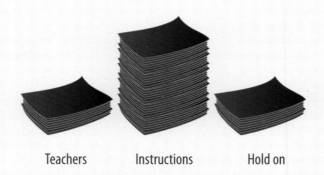

Teachers   Instructions   Hold on

Verses full of healthy teaching

In this letter, Paul gives Timothy some *healthy teaching* that he can use to effectively confront the false teachers and help the believers grow in their faith. Here are a few of these nourishing words:

This is a trustworthy saying… "Christ Jesus came into the world to save sinners." **1 Timothy 1:15**

God our Savior… wants everyone to be saved and to understand the truth. **2:3-4**

There is only one God and one Mediator who can reconcile God and humanity—the man Christ Jesus. **2:5**

The household of God. This is the church of the living God, which is the pillar and foundation of the truth. **3:15**

Without question, this is the great mystery of our faith: Christ was revealed in a human body. **3:16**

(Food) is made acceptable by the Word of God and prayer. **4:5**

Physical training is good, but training for godliness is much better. **4:8**

We brought nothing with us when we came into the world, and we can't take anything with us when we leave it. **6:7**

People who long to be rich fall into temptation. **6:9**

For the love of money is the root of all kinds of evil. **6:10**

Fight the good fight for the true faith. Hold tightly to the eternal life. **6:12**

Their trust should be in God, who richly gives us all we need. **6:17**

How to navigate 1 Timothy

1. **Meet Timothy**

   A great way for you to start your exploration of this letter is to meet its namesake, Timothy. You can read about him in the verses listed at the end of this section. In brief, Timothy was Paul's young assistant and closest co-worker, his *son in the faith,* who traveled with Paul for over 15 years. Born into a Christian family, Timothy was Biblically educated, a quick learner and was fiercely loyal to Paul (See Acts 16:1-5, 2 Tim 1:1-5, 2 Tim 3:14-15, Philippians 3:19-22).

2. **Feel Timothy's need for encouragement**

   As a large metropolitan church in a world capital, the church in Ephesus had a significant number of difficult people to corral and thorny issues to resolve. And as a 30-year old interim church leader, Timothy was not only young in age and inexperienced in leadership, but his low self-esteem often caused him to shrink back. For this reason, Paul goes out of his way to encourage, charge and challenge Timothy. Look for this.

3. **Study the qualifications for church leadership**

   In chapter three, Paul lists the prerequisites for spiritual leadership in a local church. Here he speaks of two roles: oversight and service. The *bishops*, as they were sometimes called in the Bible, were not the bishops we think of today, with lofty positions and flowing robes, but were simple leaders with responsibility for oversight of church affairs. The *deacons* were the folks who stepped up to the plate to serve the needs of the church.

Unique things about 1 Timothy

Did you know...

Paul sings the *incarnation hymn*

Paul summarizes the key pieces of Christ's life and ministry in a short, six-line praise poem that was probably sung in the early churches (1 Timothy 3:16). Here Jesus' incarnation, human life, resurrection and ascension are presented in three pairs of opposites: flesh–spirit / angels–nations / world–glory.

Real widows versus *not-so-real* widows

In the Bible, widows are special to God, and worthy of special care, since without husbands to support them they are particularly vulnerable, needy and hopeless. This church kept a list of *real* widows, older women with no family, so the church could know whom to support financially. Some *not-so-real* widows, who had families that should have supported them (but didn't), somehow appeared on the list (1 Timothy 5:3-8). Paul asked Timothy to sort this out.

We've got dancing dolphins

It was Paul's intention to return to Ephesus quickly. But fearing a delay, he wrote this letter to tell Timothy how to *behave* as the church's leader in his absence. In classical Greek usage, this word *behave* meant to move like a dolphin: to swim up and down in beautiful, delicate circles, gracefully, precisely and intentionally. Paul urged Timothy to lead the church the same way.

Recap

- 1 Timothy is a coaching conversation between Paul and Timothy during the most important *game* of Timothy's life.

- This letter provides lessons in leadership and itemizes the requirements for spiritual leaders.

- Paul challenges Timothy to step up his game and to hold on until he can get there to relieve him.

Read it!

- Read 1 Timothy now. At a casual reading pace, it will take you 13 minutes.

Self-study / Group discussion questions

- Paul mentions faith and being faithful 24 times in this short letter. Why does he do this? What is Paul trying to say? Why is faith so important to Timothy's circumstances?

- In 1 Timothy 3:1-7, Paul lists 15 qualifications for overseers. Why is each of these things important? How does being a parent help qualify a person for church leadership?

- By the tone of this letter, do you think that Paul is concerned that Timothy might run away from his assignment? Why or why not?

Insights that we can apply today

Cling to your faith in Christ, and keep your conscience clear. For some...violated their consciences...their faith has been shipwrecked.

—1 Timothy 1:18-19

Faith and a good conscience are best friends. They go together and take care of each other. To Christians, faith is our belief in Christ and in his truth. It is also our ability to believe. Conscience, on the other hand, is our God-given capacity to know right from wrong, good from evil. It is our inner alarm that warns us to steer clear of moral disasters. When our faith is strong, our conscience works effectively. Conversely, when our conscience is weak, or when we intentionally ignore its warnings, our faith crashes. Do your utmost to build up both of them.

Intro to 2 Timothy

In addition to gunpowder, medicine, paper, embroidery, porcelain, printing and silk, the Chinese proudly lay claim to yet another incredible ancient invention, the magnetic compass.

As the story goes, sometime in the fifth or sixth century BC, Chinese miners were digging for copper ore when they accidentally stumbled upon magnetite, a naturally occurring magnetic mineral whose common name is lodestone. To their surprise, the Chinese noticed that this rather ordinary looking rock had an extraordinary quality: it attracted objects made of iron.

If that wasn't mystical enough for ancients, they also discovered that when lodestone was dangled in mid-air or floated in water on a small piece of wood, it magically aligned itself to point north—and south. Which is why years later, when Chinese inventors used magnetite to develop the world's first compass, it became known as a ***south pointer***.

These were strange looking gadgets: magnetic spoon-like pointers, balanced and swiveling on square cast-bronze plates. Since magnets always point to the North Star, the pointers were made in the shape of ladles to mimic their Mama, the Big Dipper, that gigantic spoon in the sky.

Compasses soon became indispensible tools for direction, alignment and navigation. "When the people of Zheng go out to collect jade," said a 4th century BC Chinese writer, "they carry a south pointer with them so as not to lose their way." Architects used them to orient buildings, advancing the practice of Feng Shui. And mariners wouldn't leave port without them.

Four hundred years later, as Paul sat down to write this second letter to Timothy, he shared the Chinese people's love for the compass. As a prisoner of Rome who was about to be executed for crimes against the state, Paul wanted to leave Timothy a means to direct, align and navigate his life when he was gone. This letter became Timothy's south pointer.

"When I'm no longer here," wrote Paul, "continue in the direction you are now heading, following the things you have learned and been assured of. Use the Scriptures to guide your steps and to navigate life's storms. And always align yourself directly towards Jesus. He's your North Star."

2 Timothy's theme:
Goodbye for now

2 Timothy

Writer   Paul
Date written   AD 67
Place written   Rome
Recipient   Timothy
Theme   Goodbye for now

The time of my death is near. I have fought the good fight, I have finished the race, and I have remained faithful.   —2 Timothy 4:6-7

As we pick up the action, it's now five years since Paul wrote his first letter to Timothy. He has used this extended period of freedom to travel the world spreading the gospel of Jesus Christ to anyone who would listen.

But all of a sudden, things have gone horribly wrong. Caesar Nero has gone stark raving mad, torching his own capital city and accusing Christ followers of setting the fires. His henchmen are out beating the bushes for Christian leaders to capture, hogtie and feed to the lions.

Paul too is swept up in this crackdown. Some say that while working in Greece he is turned in to local authorities by Alexander the coppersmith (that jealous snitch) and is hurried back to Rome to stand trial for treason. At his pre-trial hearing, no one shows up to vouch for his innocence.

Now back in jail, only Luke, *the beloved physician*, is with him. Paul knows that he is facing certain death, but he's not afraid. The executioner's sword will be his first class, one-way ticket to heaven.

Paul's thoughts turn to Timothy, his spiritual son, who is probably still in Ephesus. Paul wants to see him one more time before his departure, both to say goodbye and to commission his ministry to him. In the dim light of the cold dungeon, Paul writes to Timothy, urging him to guard the precious truth of Christ after his death and to come quickly to Rome, while he's still alive.

Paul knows that for Timothy this may be a suicide mission. Droves of Christians have fled from Rome's heat to safe havens elsewhere. Or have disappeared underground. He also knows that Timothy is fearful by nature. Yet Christ is incredibly capable to strengthen, to protect. "Come quickly," Paul urges, "and bring Mark and my overcoat with you."

A brief outline of the letter

In 2 Timothy, Paul is in a pensive mood, thinking back on the past and looking forward to the future. As he reflects on his accomplishments, he reminisces about the experiences he and Timothy have shared in Christ's service. He then looks ahead, anticipating the day when he meets Jesus face to face and hears the words, "Well done, good and faithful servant."

	Chapters
Looking back—where I've been	1-2
Looking ahead—where I'm going	3-4

Looking back   Looking ahead

Verses that direct, align and navigate

This letter contains the last words written by Paul in the New Testament. He leaves these words of inspiration, wisdom, direction and advice as his parting gift to Timothy.

I remind you to fan into flames the spiritual gift God gave you. **2 Timothy 1:6**

God has not given us a spirit of fear and timidity, but of power, love and self-discipline. **1:7**

Hold on to the pattern of wholesome teaching you learned from me. **1:13**

Timothy, my dear son, be strong through the grace that God gives you in Christ Jesus. **2:1**

Endure suffering along with me, as a good soldier of Jesus Christ. **2:3**

Always remember that Jesus Christ, a descendant of King David, was raised from the dead. **2:8**

Work hard so you can present yourself to God and receive his approval. **2:15**

Run away from anything that stimulates youthful lusts. **2:22**

You must remain faithful to the things you have been taught. **3:14**

All Scripture is inspired by God and is useful to teach us what is true. **3:16**

Preach the word of God. Be prepared, whether the time is favorable or not. **4:2**

Keep a clear mind in every situation. Don't be afraid of suffering for the Lord. **4:5**

How to navigate 2 Timothy

1. **Feel Paul's sense of urgency**

   As Paul writes this letter, he is chained like a criminal in a Roman dungeon. And though his execution is imminent, he remains confident, knowing that he will soon be with Jesus. Yet, Timothy is far away, and there's not much time left. As you read Paul's words, feel his sense of urgency and his desire to see Timothy one last time. "Please come as soon as you can."

2. **Understand Paul's heart**

   Notice that two things occupy Paul's thoughts as he writes. Above all, he prays for Timothy, that he would live intentionally, stay strong and fulfill his calling after his departure. But Paul is also concerned about the future of God's mission on earth and, for this reason, charges Timothy to get out there and spread the word. Watch for these two major themes.

3. **Notice Paul's warnings**

   In 2 Timothy 3:1-17, Paul warns that "difficult times" will soon be coming. Not only has the Roman Empire stepped up its persecution of Christians, but people have also become shallow, selfish and ungodly. Notice how Paul steers Timothy back to his roots: faith in God and the Bible.

4. **Witness the changing of the guard**

   At this point in his life, Paul has "fought the good fight, finished the race and remained faithful." His lap is over. It's time to pass the baton to Timothy and Mark, the next generation of Christian workers. Paul urges Timothy to grab Mark and come to Rome ASAP for the hand-off.

Unique things about 2 Timothy

Did you know...

Famous people visited Paul in jail

During his imprisonment, Paul received three local celebrities, his Christian friends Pudens, Claudia and Linus (2 Timothy 4:21). According to tradition, Pudens was the son of a Roman Senator, his wife Claudia was the daughter of a British king, and, following Paul's execution, Linus became an elder in the church in Rome. During their visit, all three sent greetings to Timothy.

Soldiers, athletes and farmers

In 2 Timothy 2:3-7, Paul uses a unique, compound metaphor to triple-charge Timothy to hunker down and focus in the midst of incredibly challenging and distracting circumstances. "Be like all these guys," says Paul, "a battle-hardened soldier, a disciplined Olympic athlete and a tireless farmer."

A coat, books and parchments

Weeks away from the end of his life, Paul practices what he preaches as he hunkers down and focuses in the midst of *his* incredibly challenging and distracting circumstances. As he closes this letter, he reminds Timothy to bring his warm overcoat when he comes (it gets cold in the dungeon) along with his books (possibly Luke's writings or Jesus' words) and the parchments (probably the Old Testament) so he can continue his work till the end.

The victor's wreath

At the ancient Olympic games, instead of gold medals, winners were awarded victor's crowns to acknowledge their triumphant performances. These *crowns* were not actually crowns—they were laurel wreaths—head gear made of hand-woven branches. Based on his life of exemplary service to King Jesus, Paul was confident that he had won his.

Recap

- 2 Timothy is like a compass. Its wisdom and advice directs our lives, aligns our behaviors and helps us navigate the storms of life.

- This letter was written shortly before Paul's death. It contains the last inspired words he left us. Think of it as his last will and testament.

- Paul wanted Timothy to carry on his work and urged him to come quickly to Rome for the hand-off.

Read it!

- Read 2 Timothy now. At a casual reading pace, it will take you 9 minutes.

Self-study / Group discussion questions

- In 2 Timothy 2:1-7, Paul uses the triple metaphor of a combat soldier, an Olympic athlete and a diligent farmer to convey the idea of focusing on the tasks at hand. Read these verses. Which of these three images speaks most to you? Why?

- Imagine that you are Timothy and that Paul is your spiritual father. You have just received this letter from Paul asking you to drop everything and come to Rome immediately. You know that Nero is feeding Christians to the lions in Rome. What would you do? Why?

- In 2 Timothy 3:12, Paul says that all who desire to live godly in Christ will suffer persecution. Do you believe this? Have you suffered persecution for Christ? How?

Insights that we can apply today

This is why I remind you to fan into flames the spiritual gift God gave you. —2 Timothy 1:6

What does *fan into flame* mean? It means that though the coals are hot and the fire is alive there are no visible flames. And because there are no visible flames, the fire isn't burning with intensity. There's not much heat or light being produced. Yes, it's true that once the flame of God's Spirit ignites your spirit, it can never be extinguished. This is the gift of God. Yet whether your spirit is on fire or not is up to you. You need to take the initiative to blow on the coals. For this reason I remind *you* to fan into flame the gift of God, which is in *you*.

Intro to Titus

GASSI TOUIL, ALGERIA, 1962—In a desolate region of northern Africa, some 400 miles of windblown sand south of Algiers, a monstrous gas well fire rages out of control. Its towering flames shoot 700 feet into the air and burn with such ferocity that the fire creates its own weather. Astronaut John Glenn can see the blaze from his spacecraft as he orbits the globe.

At the wellhead, temperatures in the thousands of degrees Fahrenheit incinerate the sand piles, instantly turning them into liquid glass. The intense back pressure created by the venting of huge volumes of natural gas sucks everything in close proximity towards the mouth of the beast.

As the mighty inferno burns unabated, it consumes 550 million cubic feet of gas every day. In the six months since static electricity set the site ablaze, "**The Devil's Cigarette Lighter**," as the fire's called, has already burned up enough fuel to heat every home and business in New Hampshire and Vermont for a full year. Sitting atop the largest known gas field on the planet, this fire could continue to burn for centuries. Most oil people believe it will.

Most, that is, except Red Adair, a brash, cocky Houston-born World War II vet who has turned the bomb disposal skills he developed in the Army into an equally-dangerous peacetime profession: extinguishing oil field fires.

Red especially thrives on the impossible ones, which is exactly why he and his team are here in Algeria. They have been working non-stop at this God-forsaken site for months, drilling water wells, constructing reservoirs, clearing away melted metal debris and preparing to attack the fire head on.

On the Lighter's D-Day, Red's team floods the area with thousands of gallons of water before detonating a 750-pound nitroglycerine bomb near the wellhead. With an ear-splitting KER-BOOM, the bomb consumes all the available oxygen, snuffing out the fire like a kid blowing out birthday candles.

In a different place, and at a different time, another impossible crisis is raging out of control. This one's a thousand miles away on the island of Crete, where a group of belligerent windbags is wreaking havoc on the Christian churches of the island. Instinctively, Paul knows just the person to call to snuff out these flames. His name is Titus. He is the Bible's Red Adair.

Titus' theme:
Cleaning up a Cretan mess

Titus

Writer	Paul
Date written	AD 66
Place written	Nicopolis, Greece
Recipient	Titus
Theme	Cleaning up a Cretan mess

I left you on the island of Crete so you could complete our work there.

—Titus 1:5

The close relationship that Paul and Titus enjoyed began 16 years before the writing of this letter when Paul brought Titus, a Greek living in Antioch, to faith in Christ. Titus' conversion was so impressive that he became the poster child for Gentile Christians. In fact, Paul paraded him into a Church meeting in Jerusalem as living proof that non-Jews can be Christians too.

In the years that followed, Titus traveled extensively with Paul, eagerly spreading Christ's message throughout Asia Minor and Greece. He soon became one of Paul's most trusted co-workers and his go-to guy.

On one occasion, when a rebellion erupted in the church in Corinth, Paul shipped Titus there. "Other attempts at reconciliation having failed," write Bible scholars Philip Comfort and Walter Elwell, "he sent Titus to Corinth to try to repair the breach." And repair it he did. His remarkable success earned him the reputation of being a gutsy church troubleshooter.

This is why, shortly after Paul's release from prison, he took Titus to Crete, a rugged island off the southern coast of Greece, and dropped him off there. His task: to shut down a group of blustery agitators, bring order to many frazzled congregations and develop leaders in every church.

This promised to be a Herculean task since Cretans were by nature strong-willed, fiercely independent people who were variously characterized by others as being deceitful, drunken, gluttonous, egotistical, quarrelsome, law-breaking sluggards who were prone to start verbal fights in church.

This is why Paul wrote this letter to Titus—to remind him of these things—and to let him know that reinforcements were on the way.

A brief outline of the letter

Unlike his letters to Timothy, Paul does not need to bolster Titus' resolve or exhort him to hang in there. Rather, he simply reminds him of two areas that require attention within the churches. First, the false teachers must be silenced, and their false teachings must be corrected. Then, the ungodly behaviors of the Cretan believers must be adjusted. Not easy tasks.

	Chapters
Truth issues—what to fix and how	1
Behavioral issues—who to fix and how	2-3

Truth issues   Behavioral issues

Verses that highlight Titus' tough assignment

In this letter, Paul minces no words. He lays it all out there as he describes the difficult people who populate (and have infiltrated) the Cretan churches.

I left you on the island of Crete so you could complete our work there. **Titus 1:5**

For there are many rebellious people who engage in useless talk and deceive others. **1:10**

They must be silenced because they are turning whole families away from the truth. **1:11**

"The people of Crete are all liars, cruel animals, and lazy gluttons." **1:12**

So reprimand them sternly to make them strong in the faith. **1:13**

Teach the older men to exercise self-control. **2:2**

Similarly, teach the older women to live in a way that honors God. **2:3**

In the same way, encourage the young men to live wisely. **2:6**

Remind the believers to submit to the government and its officers. **3:1**

They must not slander anyone and must avoid quarreling. **3:2**

Do not get involved in foolish discussions...or in quarrels and fights. **3:9**

Our people must learn to do good by meeting the urgent needs of others. **3:14**

How to navigate Titus

1. **Meet Titus**

    Titus is mentioned by name quite often in the New Testament, especially in the letter of 2 Corinthians. By studying the verses listed below, an image will emerge of a Christian worker who is fearless, trustworthy, tactful, firm, wise, loyal and strong. Titus, though well-known, is not mentioned in the book of Acts at all, causing speculation that he might be Luke (the writer's) brother. (2 Cor 2:13, 7:6-15, 8:6-24, 12:16-18, Gal 2:1-3, Titus 1:4, 3:12, 2 Tim 4:10)

2. **Visualize the opposite**

    In chapter 2, Paul instructs Titus to teach the Cretan believers how to live their lives according to the healthy teachings of Scripture. As you read this chapter, Cretan conduct will come to life if you picture the opposite of what you read. "Teach the older men to exercise self control" (2:2) means that the older men are out of control. That the older women "must not be heavy drinkers" (2:3) implies that some of them are drunks. And on you go.

3. **Study the lists**

    In this letter, Paul creates four lists of important human behaviors, attitudes and actions. These lists describe virtuous, Christ-worthy conduct and point out moral and social deficiencies. Study and learn from them. Here they are:

    - The qualifications for church leadership **Titus 1:5-9**

    - Descriptions of false teachers (in general) and Cretans (in particular) **1:10-16**

    - Christian virtues for different groups of believers **2:1-10**

    - Proper social conduct for Christians **3:1-3,9**

Unique things about Titus

Did you know...

Cretans were Cretans

In Titus 1:12-13, Paul illustrates the morally repugnant behaviors of the Cretans by quoting Epimenides, a poet, philosopher and religious teacher from Crete. Six hundred years before Christ, Epimenides described his own people this way: "The people of Crete are all liars, cruel animals, and lazy gluttons."

Paul quotes five trustworthy sayings

In his letters to Timothy and Titus, Paul inserts five faithful sayings: well known, easy to remember maxims of his day that capsulize some aspect of Christian truth. Each time Paul introduces one of these axioms he uses the words, "This is a trustworthy saying," an expression that is found nowhere else in the Bible. Here are the five sayings: 1 Tim 1:15, 3:1, 4:9, 2 Tim 2:11, Titus 3:8.

Jesus Christ is God

If you're looking for one Bible verse that clearly and explicitly proves the deity of Jesus, you've come to the right place. As Paul ends this letter, he speaks of Christ's second coming in this special way: "that wonderful day when the glory of our great God and Savior, Jesus Christ, will be revealed" (Titus 2:13). In other words, Jesus Christ is our great God. There you go. Any questions?

Lies, lies and no lies

In ancient times, "to act like a Cretan," meant to lie. Though it's unclear how this island practice evolved, according to the Bible, the practice comes from the devil, the father of lies (John 8:44). For this reason, Paul draws a line in the sand, declaring that he serves "God—who does not lie" and that he helps God's people with "their knowledge of the truth."

Recap

- Titus is the Bible's Red Adair, a fearless Christian troubleshooter who is not afraid to jump into crises for the furtherance of God's kingdom.

- Paul wrote this letter to remind Titus of the objectives of his mission.

- In Titus, Paul provides four lists of behaviors believers can learn from.

Read it!

- Read Titus now. At a casual reading pace, it will take you 5 minutes.

Self-study / Group discussion questions

- At 65 words in length, Paul's self-introduction in Titus 1:1-3 is by far the longest of any of his letters, except Romans. Most of the others are from 3-20 words long. Why do you think this is? What is Paul doing here?

- In this short letter, Paul asks Titus to encourage the believers to get out there and do good works five times (1:16, 2:6, 3:1,8,14). Why? What does this say about the Cretan believers and about Christian conduct?

- Tradition says that Titus spent the rest of his life on Crete ministering to the churches there. Why? What would have caused him to do that?

Insights that we can apply today

I have been sent... to teach them to know the truth... that they have eternal life... which God promised. —Titus 1:1-2

In the opening lines of this letter, Paul says that his life's calling, the work of spreading the kingdom of God, is based on the hope of eternal life. "This word hope means different things to different people," says Bible teacher Philip Towner. "Often the way we use it—'I hope tomorrow will be a nice day,' 'I hope I get the job'—implies uncertainty. But Christian hope has an entirely different quality about it, for it is grounded on the promises of God." It is certain that God's people will enjoy eternal life. It is his will. Do you have eternal life? You can. All you need to do is to believe in Jesus and ask.

Intro to Philemon

One of the most gripping scenes in the history of major motion pictures is the galley slave sequence in William Wyler's 1959 blockbuster, *Ben Hur*. Winner of a record 11 Academy Awards, ***Ben Hur*** is the epic story of the struggle of Jewish life in Palestine, under the crushing tyranny of the Roman Empire, told from the point of view of Judah Ben Hur, a rich Jewish prince.

Condemned to a life of slavery for a crime he didn't commit, Ben Hur (played by Charlton Heston) is exiled to the raunchy bowels of a Roman galley—a naval warship propelled by 200 prisoners. There he is chained to an oar for three years, his bristling hatred for the Romans keeping him alive.

In the classic 3-minute galley sequence, Roman Admiral Quintus Arrius (played by Jack Hawkins) pushes his slaves to the threshold of death by forcing them, whip in hand, to row faster, and faster, and faster, and faster.

As the chief of the rowers pounds out the unrelenting stroke cadence with leather mallets—a driving musical score building to crescendo—Arrius calls out, "Battle speed, hortator… Attack speed… RAMMING SPEED…." Sweat pours off Ben Hur and the rest of the half-naked wretches as the rowing intensifies. With each stroke, tension becomes more excruciating (stop this! I can't watch anymore) and the result is cinematic history.

And though the circumstances of this scene are completely fictitious—the Roman navy never used prisoners—the movie's portrayal of the harsh treatment of first century slaves was painfully accurate. Back then, "slaves were not legally considered persons," says Bible teacher John MacArthur, "but were considered the tools of their masters. As such, they could be bought, sold, inherited, exchanged or seized to pay their master's debt."

Runaway slaves could be beaten or executed—a fact that weighed heavily on Paul as he sat down to write this letter to his Christian friend Philemon, whose runaway slave Onesimus, was at that very instant sitting next to Paul. Will God's love, planted in Philemon's heart, move him to forgive his slave and welcome him back? Will Paul's words persuade Philemon to do the right thing? Or will things turn out very, very badly….

Philemon's theme:
You owe me one

Philemon

Writer	Paul
Date written	AD 63
Place written	Rome
Recipient	Philemon
Theme	You owe me one

It seems Onesimus ran away for a little while so that you could have him back forever. —Philemon 15

In this one-page memo, the most private of his writings, Paul hammers away relentlessly at one central idea: forgiveness, forgiveness, forgiveness. Our favorite apostle's sole purpose for sending this letter is to urge his friend, Philemon, to forgive someone for something awful that has taken place. The curious thing is that Paul wants this to happen so badly that in 25 verses he gives Philemon 28 reasons why he should do exactly as Paul says.

The story goes this way. Philemon is a highly respected church leader who lives in the city of Colossae. Local believers gather regularly in his rather large home for worship and Bible study. There, one or more household slaves serve them, which suggests that their host is rather well to do.

One day, for some still unknown reason, Onesimus, one of the slaves, steals something that belongs to his master and runs away, heading west. Eventually, he ends up a thousand miles away in Rome, where among the unwashed multitudes, he can become invisible. Or so he thinks.

By divine coincidence, Onesimus bumps into Paul who happens to be in town at the time, awaiting trial. Before long, Paul brings our runaway to faith in Christ, and, instantly, the slave becomes a full-fledged Christian brother. To his surprise, Paul learns that Onesimus came from Colossae and served under his good friend Philemon, whom Paul also brought to faith (hmm…).

Over time, Paul and his new Christian "son" develop a close and loving relationship, yet the issues Onesimus caused in Colossae remain. For this reason, Paul urges him to go back to make things right and endorses him by writing this letter of introduction. To strongly encourage Philemon to receive his new brother, he confidently calls in a favor: "Philemon, you owe me one."

How to navigate Philemon

Paul gives Philemon 28 reasons to forgive Onesimus. Here they are, in Paul's own words (paraphrased):

1. Timothy is with me—he supports what I'm asking you to do. **Philemon 1:1**
2. You're our dear friend—don't let us down. **1:1**
3. Just in case, I'm telling Apphia, Archippus and the entire church. **1:2**
4. I am praying for you—that you will do the right thing. **1:4**
5. You love all believers: this now includes Onesimus, your new brother. **1:5**
6. Make your faith active by sharing it (with Onesimus). **1:6**
7. This is how you will discover the goodness that's inside of you. **1:6**
8. We have great joy and consolation in your love—don't ruin it for us. **1:7**
9. I could command you to do your duty: but I'd rather ask a favor. **1:8-9**
10. I am Paul. You DO understand who's asking you to do this, right? **1:9**
11. I am quite a bit older and wiser than you are. Better listen up. **1:9**
12. And I'm in jail, for Pete's sake—help me out here. **1:9**
13. Onesimus has become a Christian. He's now my spiritual son. **1:10**
14. Once he was useless—now he is extremely useful, to both of us. **1:11**
15. Receive him back as you would receive my own heart. **1:12**
16. Onesimus is helping me on your behalf—since you couldn't come. **1:13**
17. I'd like to keep him here with me—he's been such a great resource. **1:13**
18. I'm trusting that your good deed might be voluntary. **1:14**
19. He was separated from you for a while. Now he's coming back forever. **1:15**
20. He's more than a slave now—he's your true Christian brother. **1:16**
21. As a believer, he'll be much more useful to you than he was before. **1:16**
22. Do you consider me your partner? Then welcome him as you would me. **1:17**
23. If he wronged you or owes you, put it on my account. I'll pay you back. **1:18**
24. Besides all of these many reasons, you owe me one, pal. **1:19**
25. Do this favor for me, as you would do it for Christ. **1:20**
26. I have tremendous confidence that you will do what I ask. **1:21**
27. In fact, I know that you will do even more than I say. **1:21**
28. Prepare me a guest room. I'm coming to make sure all goes well. **1:22**

Unique things about Philemon

Philemon is a family affair

Paul addresses this letter to three people—Philemon (his beloved friend and co-worker), Apphia (who was probably Philemon's wife and who, most likely, helped manage the household slaves), and Archippus (who may have been their son). Their home was one of the church's meeting places.

Many Roman slaves were highly educated

Contrary to popular belief, slaves in the Roman Empire were used for more than manual labor. In addition to farming and construction work, slaves ran retail stores and were trained to be architects, sculptors, musicians, poets, librarians and physicians. For this reason, some think that Luke, the beloved physician, may have been a freed slave before becoming Paul's co-worker.

Profitable, unprofitable, profitable, profit

The name, Onesimus, literally means worthy to be *purchased* or *profitable*. In verses 10, 11 and 20, Paul demonstrates a sense of humor as he word-plays with this name, like so: "I appeal to you for my son, Profitable, who was once unprofitable to you, but has now become profitable to you... let me have profit from you."

You gotta know when to hold 'em

In this masterpiece of verbal persuasion, Paul plays his hand beautifully, holding his two highest trump cards till near the end. Here they are:
1) Philemon, above all, you owe me one, and
2) Prepare me a guest room—I'm coming to pay you a visit. How could Philemon do anything but fold?

Recap

- Philemon is a letter that explores the relationship between a runaway slave and his master, both of whom are Christians.

- Philemon is a letter about forgiveness.

- In 25 verses, Paul gives Philemon 28 reasons why he should listen to him.

Read it!

- Read Philemon now. At a casual reading pace, it will take you 5 minutes.

Self-study / Group discussion questions

- As an apostle, Paul had the spiritual authority to command Philemon to receive Onesimus back and to forgive him. Why did he chose not to use his position in this situation? Why did he appeal to Philemon instead?

- According to Paul's writings, in God's church, all believers have equal standing before God, regardless of race, gender, age or social status. Why do we often have difficulty accepting people who are different than we are? How can we overcome this tendency?

- Human slavery existed when Paul wrote this letter, and Christians, like Philemon owned slaves, like Onesimus. Yet Paul didn't use this letter or any of his other letters to speak out publicly against slavery? Why not?

Insights that we can apply today

It seems Onesimus ran away for a little while so that you could have him back forever. —Philemon 15

Onesimus stole something from Philemon and ran away. In doing so he committed two illegal acts. Both had consequences. And while Paul does not condone Onesimus' behavior, he suggests in this verse that God used these circumstances to accomplish a higher purpose. For this reason, Paul urges Philemon to forgive Onesimus. Is there someone you need to forgive for something they've done or said to you? Perhaps God wants to do something of eternal worth with your circumstances. Why not give Him a chance to do so?

General Letters

Intro to Hebrews

OREGON, WISCONSIN—In this sleepy little town some ten miles due south of Madison, Wisconsin, not far from the junction of State Road 138 and County MM, 15 exceptionally fit women park their cars, lace up their boots and start to stretch. They meet here at Kennedy Park twice a week, or in a shed if the weather gets nasty, to practice the sport they know and love.

Meet the Oregon Tuggers, one of the world's premier women's Tug of War teams that, as perennial US National Champions, completely dominated the sport in the eighties and nineties. As it turns out, Oregon, Wisconsin, is America's tugging epicenter. "Southern Wisconsin is a hotbed for Tug of War," says **Shelby Richardson**, coach of the Tuggers and the President of the U.S. Tug of War Association. "It's a huge sport in the Midwest."

And—who would have guessed—it's a huge sport globally. Each year, thousands of male and female teams from 56 nations compete at events sponsored by the Tug of War International Federation, the sport's governing body. And every two years the world's strongest squads heave and tow against each other to determine the toughest tuggers on terra firma.

Athletic contests between two teams at opposite ends of a rope date back to antiquity. Art depicting a TOW competition has been discovered on the wall of a 4,000-year-old tomb in Egypt and in a 12th century relief at the Sun Temple of Konark in India. Ancient religious cultists tugged against one another in far-flung places like Borneo and Burma. And the sport has been featured in the Olympic Games, both in ancient Greece and in modern times.

Believe it or not, Tug of War is also pictured in the Bible, especially in our present letter, Hebrews. But here the focus is not so much on the teams, but on the rope. In Tug of War competitions, a natural fiber rope is used. In Hebrews, it's Jewish Christians who are being pulled. And the tension is mounting.

The question is, will their love of Christ, the power of God's Spirit and the urgency of this letter pull these believers forward to their heavenly destinies or will intense pressure from their Jewish families and the magnetic attraction of their former religion conspire to draw them back over the line?

Hebrew's theme:
Choose the better path

Hebrews

Writer	God only knows
Date written	AD 66
Place written	Unknown
Recipients	Jewish Christians
Theme	Choose the better path

Jesus... has been given a ministry that is far superior. —Hebrews 8:6

In the book of Exodus, as Moses was leading two million Hebrews out of slavery in Egypt, he called a halt to their freedom trek at the foot of Mt. Sinai to go up the mountain and hear from God. "I have brought you to myself," God said. "If you will follow me, you will be my special people. Deal? Deal."

Later, Moses received Ten Commandments from God, laws given to help his people live upright lives. And at a subsequent meeting, God gave Moses detailed designs for the Tabernacle, a large mobile worship center that he wanted the people to build for him in the desert (it was awesome).

To staff this facility, God asked Moses to establish a priesthood: a team of worship leaders who would bring the people's needs to him. Thus, at Mt. Sinai the Jewish religion was born, that God-given belief system, complete with laws, ceremonies and sacrifices, which served the Jews well for over 1,400 years. That is, until Christ came and inaugurated a better way.

On the cross, Jesus took away the sins of the world. So, there was no longer any need for God's people to offer sacrifices for their sins. And since Jesus offered his followers spiritual re-birth and direct contact with God, Jewish behavioral laws and ceremonial worship lost their value. Believers could now come together anytime, anywhere to worship God in spirit and in truth.

For some Jewish Christians, Christ's better way caused serious issues. Patriotic Jews harassed them for abandoning their cherished religion. And as opposition intensified, their faith began to waver. They wondered whether following Jesus was the right thing for them to do, or not.

For this reason, the writer of Hebrews drafted this strongly-worded letter, urging them to leave their past behind, focus their eyes dead ahead on the path towards Jesus, and run, run, run, never looking back.

A brief outline of the letter

Hebrews has two sections. The first is loaded with comparisons. Here, the writer shows that Christ and his ministry are superior to important things in the Jewish religion. In the second section, the writer says that the way to be free from the power of the past is to actively engage with Christ by faith.

	Chapters
Teaching: Christ is much better	
Better than angels	1-2
Better than Moses and Joshua	3-4
Better than Old Testament priests	5-7
Better than Old Testament ministry	8
Better than Old Testament sacrifices	9-10
Practice: Faith is your way forward	
Faith's history	11
Faith's challenge	12-13

Teaching   Practice

Verses that show that Christ is much better

The following verses are statements of fact that demonstrate to the wavering Jewish Christians (and to us) that Christ is much better than religion.

Through the Son, God created the universe. **Hebrews 1:2**

The Son radiates God's own glory and expresses his character. **1:3**

When he had cleansed us from our sins, he sat down in the place of honor. **1:3**

The Son is far greater than the angels. **1:4**

By God's grace, Jesus tasted death for everyone. **2:9**

We have a great High Priest who has entered heaven, Jesus the Son of God. **4:14**

He became the source of eternal salvation for all those who obey him. **5:9**

He is able, once and forever, to save those who come to God through him. **7:25**

He… mediates for us a far better covenant with God, based on better promises. **8:6**

Christ died once for all time as a sacrifice to take away sins. **9:28**

By his death, Jesus opened a new and life-giving way. **10:20**

Jesus (is) the champion who initiates and perfects our faith. **12:2**

How to navigate Hebrews

Look for the 13 encouragements (carrots)

In the original language, the writer of Hebrews uses the phrase, "Let us," 13 times to strongly encourage his readers to abandon their old religious practices and follow Jesus. Watch for them. Here they are, paraphrased:

1. Let us fear that we would come up short. **Hebrews 4:1**
2. Let us be diligent to reach God's objective. **4:11**
3. Let us hold on to our confession of faith. **4:14**
4. Let us approach God's throne of grace boldly. **4:16**
5. Let us go on toward perfection. **6:1**
6. Let us draw near to God. **10:22**
7. Let us hold on to our confession of hope. **10:23**
8. Let us think of ways to encourage each other. **10:24**
9. Let us lay aside our sins and entanglements. **12:1**
10. Let us run the race God laid out before us. **12:1**
11. Let us take grace and give thanks. **12:28**
12. Let us bear the disgrace that Jesus bore. **13:13**
13. Let us offer praise to God. **13:15**

Look for the five warnings (sticks)

In addition to 13 positive encouragements (carrots), the writer includes five negative encouragements (sticks) to help motivate his readers to action. Watch for these. Here they are, paraphrased:

1. Do not ignore God's Son. **2:1-4**
2. Do not harden your hearts towards God. **3:7-4:13**
3. Do not remain as baby Christians. **5:11-6:20**
4. Do not fall back into your old religion. **10:19-32**
5. Do not fall away from God's grace. **6:15-29**

Unique things about Hebrews

Did you know...

No one knows who wrote Hebrews

The writer does not identify himself. And while the letter's content matches Paul's theology, the writing style does not, leading some to speculate that Paul may have dictated the letter to someone else who wrote it down. Or that Barnabas, Luke, Apollos or another member of Paul's circle wrote it.

Hebrews is the Fifth Gospel

While the four Gospels (Matthew, Mark, Luke and John) record Jesus' former ministry on earth, Hebrews describes Jesus' current activities in heaven. Jesus, as our heavenly High Priest, brings our requests to God, leads us into God's presence, and supplies our need (Hebrews 7:24-28).

Hebrews showcases a history of faith

Hebrews 11 is a unique Bible chapter. Here, the writer chronicles the history of faith, often in the face of adversity, starting at God's creation and continuing up through the time of Christ. This one chapter provides an excellent overview of the power of faith in the Old Testament.

The Christian life is like riding a bicycle

Hebrews is a letter about forward motion. In many places readers are strongly urged to come forward, to draw near to God's throne, to run the race ahead of them, and not to slow down, stand still or go backwards. "The Christian life is like riding a bicycle," says Bible teacher Henrietta Mears. "If you do not go on, you go off."

Recap

- Hebrews is like a Tug of War. Jewish Christians are being pulled in two directions at the same time.

- Hebrews is a letter about forward motion—movement towards Jesus (our Captain, Pioneer and Forerunner) and away from our past lives.

- The writer of this letter uses 13 encouragements (carrots) and five warnings (sticks) to motivate his readers to take action.

Read it!

- Read Hebrews now. At a casual reading pace, it will take you 37 minutes.

Self-study / Group discussion questions

- Today, Jesus is in heaven, interceding for his followers on earth before the Father's throne. How do you picture this activity? Does he ever rest? How does this make you feel about Jesus?

- According to Hebrews 1:14 and 2:7, even though the angels are a higher race of creatures than human beings (they never feel thirst, grow old or give birth) God has directed them to assist and protect us, the believers, "those who are about to inherit salvation." How might knowing this affect your life?

- Why is it necessary for Christians to constantly move forward in their faith walk? Why is bicycle imagery a powerful illustration of the Christian life? What happens when a bicycle rider stops pedaling?

Insights that we can apply today

Let us strip off every weight... and let us run with endurance the race God has set before us... keeping our eyes on Jesus.

—Hebrews 12:1-2

In these verses, the writer of Hebrews paints a vivid picture of a relay race at the ancient Olympic Games to show modern day Christians what it's like to live for Christ. The stadium's stands are packed with former runners, believers who have finished their lap and passed on. They fully surround the runners on the track like a great cloud, loudly cheering them on. As the current racers sprint around turn four, a new group enters the stadium, takes off their sweats (and anything else that might slow them down), and prepares to grab the batons and takeoff on their own lap of life, looking heavenward to Jesus. Get ready—it's your turn to start running.

Intro to James

TUSCUMBIA, ALABAMA, 1887—Helen Keller is nearly seven. And though at times she might seem normal, she has been completely deaf, mute and blind since infancy. Over the past six years, since her parents couldn't bear to watch her cry, they have allowed Helen to do as she pleased. This has turned their pretty little girl into an uncontrollable tyrant.

Enter **Anne Sullivan**, a 20-year-old graduate of the Perkins School for the Blind who just arrived from Boston to become Helen's personal teacher. One day, Mark Twain will call Anne "the miracle worker." But before any miracles can be worked, Helen must learn to trust Anne, and Anne must teach Helen to behave. Fasten your seat belts. Here comes some tough love.

The first clouds of confrontation gather at the Keller household four days after Anne arrives. That morning, after breakfast is served, Helen gropes her way around the table, paws at each person's plate and helps herself to what she finds. As Helen reaches for Anne's dish, Anne pushes her away. When Helen explodes, Anne dismisses the family and locks the door.

"Helen was lying on the floor," Anne later recalls, "kicking and screaming and trying to pull my chair from under me. She kept this up for half an hour, then got up… I let her see that I was eating, but did not let her put her hand in the plate. She pinched me, and I slapped her every time she did it…"

"After a few minutes she came back to her place and began to eat her breakfast with her fingers. I gave her a spoon, which she threw on the floor. I forced her out of her chair and made her pick it up. Finally, I succeeded in getting her back in her chair again…"

Within days, as the battles subsided and communication breakthroughs started coming, an amazing transformation began to occur. And over time, because of Anne's tenacious, self-sacrificial love for this spoiled little girl, Helen Keller became one of the most remarkable women in history.

In another land, at another time, another tough lover looks for a miracle. His self-indulged spiritual children are behaving badly and desperately need a spanking. So he picks up his pen and begins to write a firm but friendly letter to them: "James… to the… Jewish believers scattered abroad. Greetings!"

James' theme:
Step up

James

Writer   James
Date written   AD 50
Place written   Jerusalem
Recipients   Jewish Christians outside of Palestine
Theme   Step up

Unless (faith) produces good deeds, it is dead and useless.

—James 2:17

There are four different James' mentioned in the New Testament. The one who wrote this letter was Jesus' half-brother, who, oddly enough, didn't believe that Jesus was the Savior during the many months and years that they washed dishes and did carpentry together under the same roof in Nazareth.

Fortunately for him, James became a believer sometime after Christ's resurrection, when Jesus paid him a visit, tapped him on the shoulder and said, "Hi brother. Guess what?"

From then on, James became a fiercely loyal follower of Christ and soon emerged as a strong leader in the newly formed Church in Jerusalem. When Peter left to work for Christ in other parts of the country, James became the de facto leader of the church and the most influential Christian in Palestine.

For years, he channeled his energies into meeting the needs of Christian brothers and sisters across the region and beyond, most of whom were converts from Judaism. This letter was written to them.

In it, James expresses concern for two things. First, he is quite bothered that so many of the Christians he comes in contact with speak and behave exactly like unbelievers. Shouldn't there be huge differences? You bet there should. So James challenges his readers to live uplifted, God-pleasing lives by following Jesus' teachings, some of which he then summarizes for them.

James is also convinced that the faith of many believers is too shallow. He argues that if people's faith in Christ is deeply rooted, their daily lives should abound with works of charity, especially towards the poor, widows and orphans. That he is not seeing evidence of this is a huge problem.

A brief outline of the letter

Since James covers so many different topics, it is difficult to outline his letter. Yet it can be roughly separated into three parts, as follows:

	Chapters
Real religion—helping orphans and widows	1:1-27
Real faith—a changed, outward-focused life	2:1-3:12
Real wisdom—heavenly, pure, full of mercy	3:13-5:20

Real religion   Real faith   Real wisdom

Verses that contain imperatives

In this five-chapter letter (108 verses), James uses 54 action verbs, like, *consider, ask, do, don't, come close, humble, confess, pray* and so forth. James is urging the believers to do something with their faith. As you read this letter, look for these. Better still, get a pen and write them down.

When troubles come your way, consider it an opportunity for great joy. **James 1:2**

If you need wisdom, ask our generous God, and he will give it to you. **1:5**

Do not waver, for a person with divided loyalty is as unsettled as a wave. **1:6**

Don't be misled...Whatever is good and perfect comes down to us from God our Father. **1:16**

Don't just listen to God's word. You must do what it says. **1:22**

If you are wise and understand God's ways, prove it by living an honorable life. **3:13**

Resist the devil, and he will flee from you. **4:7**

Come close to God, and God will come close to you. **4:8**

Humble yourselves before the Lord, and he will lift you up in honor. **4:10**

Don't speak evil against each other, dear brothers and sisters. **4:11**

Don't grumble about each other, brothers and sisters, or you will be judged. **5:9**

Confess your sins to each other and pray for each other so that you may be healed. **5:16**

How to navigate James

1. **Know that this letter reads like a collection of proverbs**

   This letter is often characterized as the Proverbs of the New Testament. It contains dozens of wise sayings, axioms to help our everyday lives. So, it doesn't read like a story, or a biography, or a normal letter. Rather, it reads like a series of short sermons linked together.

2. **Think about the relationship between faith and deeds**

   Read James 2:14-26. Here, James *seems* to say that for a person to be accepted by God, faith is insufficient: deeds are also needed. This *seems* to fly in the face of what Paul teaches in Romans or Galatians: that people are saved by faith in Christ alone. Truth is, the two writers complement one another. We *are* made right with God by faith in Christ alone, and real faith naturally produces good deeds. When it doesn't, there's a problem.

3. **Notice James' heart for justice**

   James supports social activism more than most other Bible writers. In this letter, he urges his readers to help the poor, clothe and feed the destitute, visit the orphans and widows. Look for this recurring theme as you read.

4. **Watch for James' references to nature**

   James must have really loved the great outdoors since his writing makes so many references to nature. His proverbial sayings include wind and waves, land and sea, flowers and grass, forests and trees, rain and fog, harvest and seeds, birds and fish, olives and figs, and so much more.

Unique things about James

Did you know. . .

There are four James' in the New Testament

Two are well known; two, not so much. The most famous James is John's older brother, one of Jesus' 12 apostles. Religious radicals murdered him in AD 44. The two lesser knowns are James, the son of Alphaeus, (also one of Jesus' 12 apostles), and James, father of Judas (not Iscariot). The other prominent James is Jesus' half-brother, the writer of this letter.

James quotes Jesus all over the place

There are significant parallels between Jesus' teachings and the lessons taught by his half-brother James in this letter. Here, James reproduces over 20 of Jesus' sayings from his famous Sermon on the Mount (Matthew 5-7). And in five short chapters, he passes on more of Jesus' words than can be found in the rest of the New Testament letters combined.

The demons are freaking out

In James 2:19, our writer points out that to believe that there is one God is a good thing. Yet that belief is pretty basic: "Even the demons believe this, and they *tremble* in terror." The word translated tremble is *phrisso*, an ancient Greek word (used only here in the Bible) which means to be frightened so badly that the hair on the back of your neck stands up.

James had camels' knees

James was a serious-minded Christian. Tradition tells us that he would often go into the temple in Jerusalem to pray on his knees, pleading for forgiveness for his Jewish countrymen. Over the years, his knees became so rough and calloused that they looked like camels' knees (ouch).

Recap

- James is a letter of tough love. In short, he wants his readers to quit playing around with the world and be real Christians.

- To James, the proof is in the pudding. He's saying, "I don't believe you! Prove it. Where's the beef? Show me."

- James is an action-oriented letter. It is filled with imperatives. James is a catalyst, and his goal is to prod the believers into taking action.

Read it!

- Read James now. At a casual reading pace, it will take you 13 minutes.

Self-study / Group discussion questions

- In Genesis 3, God practiced tough love by disciplining Adam and Eve and by chasing them out of the Garden of Eden. Although God is gracious, why does he often use tough love to deal with his people?

- James 5:16 promises that, "The earnest prayer of a righteous person... produces wonderful results." In your own words, what is an earnest prayer? What does it mean to pray fervently? How is praying fervently different from your normal prayers? Describe the qualities of a righteous person. Why does James link righteousness with effectiveness?

- Why did James use a Proverbs-style of writing rather than the "normal" way of writing a letter? Why is his writing organized in this particular way?

Insights that we can apply today

Come close to God, and God will come close to you. —James 4:8

In Old Testament times, according to the way God set things up for his people, only priests could approach God and come into his presence. But two thousand years ago, by his death on the cross, Jesus Christ opened the way for everyone on the planet to draw near to God to receive his grace and mercy directly. In this verse, James suggests that even though God is always with us, in our experience, he can sometimes seem distant and far away. But when we take action to turn away from other things and open our hearts to him, we can once again sense his loving presence in our lives. There's no better time than the present. Why wait any longer?

Intro to 1 & 2 Peter

As the video rolls, a haunting melody swells as spectacular scenes of craggy snow-capped peaks fill the screen. Then you see the **sheep**—hundreds and hundreds of sheep.

Voice-over: "It is quite simply breathtaking. Towering mountains rising high above Lake Wakatibu. This is iconic New Zealand high country, and home for shepherd and musterer (sheep gatherer) Sharon Chart."

As a large flock scampers across a rocky hillside, Sharon and her five dogs emerge from behind a knoll. A pig-tailed thirty-something, Sharon looks the part, what with her down vest, fleece turtleneck, gray shorts, blue tights, leather cap and muddy hiking boots. As she walks towards the camera, a staff in her right hand, she whistles to the sheep.

Sharon: "I love it, absolutely," she says glancing towards the majestic mountains that surround her. "Every day is different. Look at where I am; this is my office; how can you beat it? It's just fantastic."

Voice-over: "Shaz, as her mates call her, is a rare breed. A woman doing a man's job." (Sharon grabs a set of tire chains and wrestles them over her truck's front wheel). "Murray and Karen Scott run Loch Linne Station just south of Queenstown near Kingston. Last year, they were without a shepherd. So, they advertised. Little did they know that a woman would apply."

So goes this delightful human-interest piece that reporter Harnish Clark filmed for 3News, a TV station in Auckland, New Zealand, in the summer of 2008. What makes the story compelling, besides the idyllic scenery and thousands of sheep, is Sharon Chart—an unusually determined shepherd who tackles a job that is difficult for most men to do and thrives at it.

In our next two letters, you'll be introduced to another unique shepherd—Simon Peter. Simon, as his mates call him, is a rare breed. A man doing Jesus' job. Just before leaving for heaven, the Chief Shepherd appointed him to feed his sheep, and for the past 30 years Peter has done just that.

What makes Peter's letters compelling, besides his rich teaching and helpful life lessons, is Simon Peter—an unusually determined shepherd who tackles a job that is difficult for most men to do and thrives at it.

1 Peter's theme:
Hang tough

1 Peter

Writer   Peter
Date written   AD 64
Place written   Rome
Recipients   Scattered Christians
Theme   Hang tough

Stand firm against (the devil), and be strong in your faith.

—1 Peter 5:9

In the four Gospels, Simon Peter comes across as an impulsive and emotional teenage disciple of Christ who seems to get it wrong as often as he gets it right.

Yet a short time later, in the opening pages of the book of Acts, a more mature Peter emerges. Here, he appears as a fearless leader of the Christian movement—a gifted twenty-something—boldly proclaiming Jesus as Lord and bringing thousands of unbelievers into God's flock.

Now in his letters, written near the end of his life, Peter is a seasoned veteran. He is about 60 years old and, for two-thirds of his life, has fought the good fight against the relentless tide of anti-Christian tyranny, mostly at the hands of radical Jews, and has the battle scars to prove it.

As Peter begins to write this *hang tough* letter to believers who are scattered across northern Asia Minor, he knows that their environment is about to change radically for the worse. Living in Rome at the time, he is witnessing this change unfold first-hand.

Caesar Nero has banned the practice of Christianity, labeling it as an anti-Roman cult. As a result, fresh waves of anti-Christian persecution have begun to radiate out through the provinces of the Empire. Soon "fiery trials," as Peter calls them, will reach the churches in Asia Minor and times will turn tough.

Before they do, Peter will warn the brothers of the storm that's headed their way and steel their resolve with Christ-sized doses of hope and encouragement. "So if you are suffering in a manner that pleases God," suggests Peter in 1 Peter 4:19, "keep on doing what is right, and trust your lives to God who created you, for he will never fail you."

A brief outline of the letter

In the first part of this letter, Peter describes the blessings God has for those who follow Him. In the second section, he compares our life in Christ to a journey and helps us stay on the path. In the last section, he presents Christ's sufferings as a model for our sufferings. Both bring glory.

	Chapters
Blessings—faith, salvation, a new birth, and so much more	1
Pilgrimage—our Christian life is a pilgrimage, a journey	2-3
Suffering—sufferings are headed our way	4-5

Blessings   Pilgrimage   Suffering

Verses that bring hope during difficult times

In this letter of hope, Peter inspires those who suffer because of their faith in Christ. These verses raise our sights heavenward and create a higher realization of what God is accomplishing through our suffering.

Through your faith, God is protecting you by his power. **1 Peter 1:5**

There is wonderful joy ahead, even though you have to endure many trials. **1:6**

These trials will show that your faith is genuine… more precious than mere gold. **1:7**

You love him even though you have never seen him. **1:8**

The reward for trusting him will be the salvation of your souls. **1:9**

You are living stones that God is building into his spiritual temple. **2:5**

You are a chosen people… royal priests… God's very own possession. **2:9**

Dear friends, don't be surprised at the fiery trials you are going through. **4:12**

Instead, be very glad—for these trials make you partners with Christ. **4:13**

Praise God for the privilege of being called by his name! **4:16**

When the Great Shepherd appears, you will receive a crown of never-ending glory. **5:4**

Give all your worries and cares to God, for he cares about you. **5:7**

How to navigate 1 Peter

1. **Underline the word** *suffering*

    In this short letter of 105 verses, Peter uses the word *suffering* 16 times. The Christians who will read this letter are social outcasts, aliens in a pagan society, persecuted for living godly lives. Notice how Peter presents Christ's suffering as a model for the believers to follow.

2. **Feel the hope**

    As you read this letter, feel the hope that Peter, "the Apostle of hope," conveys to his readers by his heartening words. Notice how hope, to Peter, is alive. It is a great expectation that emboldens the faithful to stand against adversity, assuring them that it's going to be okay.

3. **Do good deeds**

    Like James, Peter urges the believers to express their love for Christ by living right and helping the people around them. In Peter's words, "Even if they accuse you of doing wrong, they will see your honorable behavior, and they will give honor to God." Peter repeats this *do good* message eight times. Watch for these. Here they are: 1 Peter 2:12, 14, 15, 20; 3:13, 16, 17; 4:19.

Unique things about 1 Peter

Did you know...

Angels are curious little rascals...

...especially when it comes to watching Christians. When Peter says that angels "are eagerly watching" these things (1 Peter 1:12), he literally means that they are so excited to see how Christ is working in us that they stoop down, eyes wide open, and crane their necks so they won't miss a thing. Our most rabid fans are watching us from above and cheering us on.

Jesus visited the underworld

1 Peter 3:19-20 says that after Jesus died, he "went and preached to the spirits in prison—those who disobeyed God long ago." Some Bible teachers believe that this refers to a trip he took to the underworld where evil spirits from Noah's time were being held for Judgment Day. After declaring victory to them, Jesus said, "Watch this," and rose triumphantly from the dead.

Mark was Peter's "son"

Peter treated Mark as his spiritual son (5:13) in much the same way that Paul mentored Timothy (1 Tim 1:2). For years, Mark traveled with Peter, and near the end of Peter's life, wrote down his teacher's recollections of his first-hand experiences with Jesus. Quite possibly, this became the Gospel of Mark. Peter seems to refer to it in his second letter (2 Pet 1:15).

Got Word?

In trying times, Peter urges the faithful to take God's Word as their primary source of strength and spiritual nourishment. He wants all Christians to hunger for the Bible with the same eagerness and intensity as newborns crave their mothers' milk. To feed on the Word of God in this way, says Peter, is to taste the Lord Himself. And boy, does he taste good.

Recap

- When you think of this letter, imagine a shepherd reassuring his flock of fearful, scattered sheep that everything is going to be okay.

- Remember that 1 Peter is a letter of hope and a call to hang tough, regardless of what happens.

- Peter reminds us that, for Christians, God's Word is a primary source of strength and spiritual nourishment.

Read it!

- Read 1 Peter now. At a casual reading pace it will take you 14 minutes.

Self-study / Group discussion questions

- In the Bible, God's people are often compared to sheep. Why is this? What characteristics and behaviors of sheep and believers are similar? Read Psalm 23 and describe how God shepherds his sheep.

- Make a list of all the verses where the words *suffer* or *suffering* occur. What is similar or different about the context of these verses? Why does Peter believe that suffering can actually be a good thing?

- Peter opens his letter with a discussion of God's blessings and ends it with a call to stand up to suffering. Why does he structure the letter in this way? Why not open with suffering and end with God's blessings?

Insights that we can apply today

Give all your worries and cares to God, for he cares for you.

—1 Peter 5:7

It is normal for human beings to feel anxious, worried and concerned about things. Issues arise. Disappointments come. Crises happen. Yet, God has provided a positive way for us to deal with our anxious feelings. He asks us to throw them in his direction, by an act of will, and trust that he will take care of them. Open your hands. Let go of your cares. Release them from your control, and put them into God's hands, knowing that he thinks about you and cares for you. To do this is to find peace.

2 Peter's theme:

Watch out for the wolves

2 Peter

Writer	Peter
Date written	AD 64
Place written	Rome
Recipients	Scattered Christians
Theme	Watch out for the wolves

Be on guard so that you will not be carried away. . . —2 Peter 3:17

Soon after he sent his first letter from Rome, Peter learned of a new crisis brewing in Asia Minor. False teachers had started to infiltrate the churches, using deceit to take advantage of the believers financially and lies to destroy their faith in Christ.

While the "fiery trials" mentioned in 1 Peter were public events that approached with the ferocity of lions tearing into flocks, the invasion of the wolves in 2 Peter was far more subtle.

Jesus had warned his disciples to be wary of people who speak about God, but who aren't what they appear to be. "Beware of false prophets," he said, "who come disguised as harmless sheep but are really vicious wolves. You can identify them by their fruit" (Matthew 7:15).

Years later, Paul used Jesus' language to bid farewell to the elders in Ephesus: "I know that false teachers, like **vicious wolves**, will come in among you after I leave, not sparing the flock" (Acts 20:29).

Now, the wolves have invaded Peter's world. It's his turn to sound the wolf alarm. So, in his second letter (to the same recipients), Peter warns the brothers to watch out for these predators and tells them, in no uncertain terms, of the awful punishment that awaits them on Judgment Day.

But, there is also a second, more personal purpose for this letter. Things have become a bit desperate for Peter in Rome. He has been arrested and jailed, and expects to be executed soon. Like Paul's second letter to Timothy, this will be Peter's last letter, his fond farewell.

A brief outline of the letter

Peter hits three main points in this letter. First, he presents true knowledge, the knowledge of Christ, as a universal antidote against the lies of the false teachers. Then he exposes the wolves and describes the doom that awaits them. Finally, he assures the believers that though Christ seems to be delaying his return, he will fulfill his promise at God's appointed time.

	Chapters
True knowledge—the universal Christian antidote	1
False teachers—peddling heresy and immorality	2
Christ's return—a sure promise, at God's time	3

True knowledge   False teachers   Christ's return

Verses that encourage and warn

Peter brings both encouragement and warning to those being confused by false teachers. These verses give you a taste of Peter's shepherding care for the believers.

God has given us everything we need for living a godly life. **2 Peter 1:3**

We have received all of this by coming to know him. **1:3**

He has given us great and precious promises. **1:4**

These are the promises that enable you to share his divine nature. **1:5**

Make every effort to respond to God's promises. **1:5**

There will be false teachers among you. **2:1**

They will cleverly teach destructive heresies and even deny the Master. **2:1**

Many will follow their evil teaching and shameful immorality. **2:2**

In their greed they will make up clever lies to get hold of your money. **2:3**

They delight in deception even as they eat with you in your fellowship meals. **2:13**

They promise freedom, but they themselves are slaves of sin and corruption. **2:19**

Be on guard so that you will not be carried away by... these wicked people. **3:17**

How to navigate 2 Peter

1. **Realize that this is a letter of warning**

    Peter senses that danger is coming and writes to put the believers on high alert. Notice the strong, urgent, directive language he uses—"Do this. Pay attention to that. Remember this." Watch how Peter shepherds his flock by the words he chooses.

2. **Notice the role that knowledge plays**

    Peter uses the word *knowledge* 16 times in this short letter. Watch for it. This Greek word describes the kind of knowledge that comes from our experiences. It is different and deeper than mere book knowledge. The experiential knowledge of Christ prepares Christians for attacks on their faith, protects them from falling for the lies of false teachers, and prevents them from being sucked into rampant immorality.

3. **Appreciate the descriptions of false teachers**

    In chapter two, Peter uses vivid language to portray the greedy, immoral, deceptive, exploitative, ego-driven, lying, Christ-hating false teachers and the evil things they do. Then, by presenting examples of God's judgment of a few ungodly people from the Old Testament, he paints a dreadful picture of the punishment that awaits them.

Unique things about 2 Peter

Did you know…

Jesus and Peter make an "exodus"

In the Gospels, Jesus leads Peter and two others to the top of a mountain. There, in blinding light, Moses and Elijah appear out of nowhere and speak with Jesus about his upcoming *death* on the cross (Luke 9:31). Peter, remembering this, uses the same word to foretell his own *death* (2 Peter 1:15). In these two verses, the Greek word for death is *exodus*, a departure.

Peter loves to recycle his metaphors

Here are some examples: The Word is a shining light (1 Peter 2:9, 2 Peter 1:19). Noah and the flood are like salvation and judgment (1 Peter 3:20, 2 Peter 2:5). Christian lives are temporal, earthly pilgrimages (1 Peter 1:1, 2 Peter 1:13-14). Our faith, like a seed, grows and is self-sufficient (1 Peter 1:23, 2 Peter 1:3).

Peter read Paul's letters

Peter sent his two letters to believers who had previously read Paul's letters. He was familiar with Paul's writings and found some things "hard to understand" (2 Peter 3:15-16). It could be that following Paul's death, a collection of his letters had been compiled and circulated among the churches.

God is not in a hurry

2 Peter 3:8 says, "A day is like a thousand years to the Lord…" Here Peter quotes Psalm 90 to remind us of God's incredible patience and love toward us, though many continue to reject him. Said another way, "Grace, not judgment, is the leading note of God's music."

Recap

- 2 Peter is a letter of warning—watch out for the wolves.

- This letter is Peter's farewell. He expects to be executed for his faith in Christ soon.

- Experiential knowledge of Christ is a universal antidote that guards Christians against attacks on their faith.

Read it!

- Read 2 Peter now. At a casual reading pace it will take you 9 minutes.

Self-study / Group discussion questions

- After being warned by Peter that there are false teachers in their midst, how might the believers react? What actions might they take? How might their daily lives and practices change?

- 2 Peter 3:9 says that Jesus is not slow with regard to keeping his promise to return to earth. Rather, he patiently waits for people to turn in his direction, not willing that anyone should perish, but that all should be saved. What are some implications of Jesus' actions?

- To counteract the immoral life style being peddled by the false teachers, Peter urges the believers to become much more diligent in the practice of their Christian faith. What does being diligent mean to you? Do you consider yourself a diligent person? How can you become more diligent?

Insights that we can apply today

Grow in the grace and knowledge of our Lord and Savior Jesus Christ. —2 Peter 3:18

Peter ends the last sentence of his farewell letter with the idea of growth. This is because the Christian life is living and organic. Believers, birthed a second time by God himself when they receive Jesus as Lord, have a living hope planted within us—a divine seed that demands to grow. Just as nourishment and exercise turn babies into adults, just as rains and rich soil turn seeds into trees, so grace and experiential knowledge of Christ make us more Christ-like, day by day.

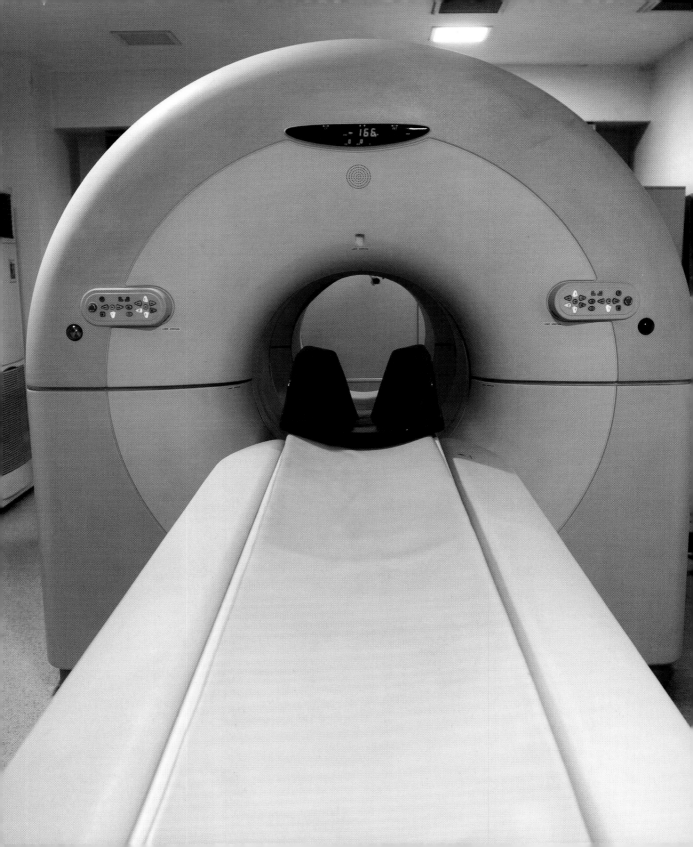

Intro to John's letters

ANNADALE, VIRGINIA, 1999—Jennifer Johnson (as we'll call her here), a 27-year-old mother of two, is recovering from the delivery of her third baby when someone urges her to pay a visit to the Metro Region PET Center a few miles outside Washington, D.C.

Though she is not really in the market for a new puppy or eager to volunteer to promote local spay and neuter programs, Jennifer follows their advice— seems she has some serious PET business to take care of.

Jennifer's doctors have referred her to this facility to determine whether melanoma, an especially deadly skin cancer, is spreading undetected in her body. Dr. Eric Norby, Metro Region's Medical Director, will use Positron Emission Tomography (PET), a new technology, to search for malignancies.

By peering directly into the body's cells, **PET scans**, as they're called, can identify areas of increased metabolic activity (hot spots) in the body. Since cancer cells have voracious appetites, scanned tumors glow brightly.

"About midway through (Jennifer's) pregnancy," recalls Dr. Norby, "she was found to have a large melanoma on her abdomen. It was very worrisome because of its depth and size." Surgeons removed the tumor and ran follow-up tests to search for other cancer in her body. They found none.

"When every conventional study came back negative," says Dr. Norby, "she was referred to us for a PET scan." This time, the scan came back positive. The cancer had metastasized to Jennifer's groin and to one of her armpits. Two new tumors had formed. These too were surgically removed.

"Usually, when a cancer has spread like this, it has gone everywhere and is very deadly," says Dr. Norby. "Had it not been for the PET scan, those two areas would have continued to grow and spread and this mother of three small children would most likely have died."

When the Apostle John wrote his letters, Gnosticism, an especially deadly form of spiritual cancer, was spreading through the churches. Dr. John created the tests contained in his three letters (the PET scanners of the New Testament) so the believers could identify areas of increased evil activity (hot spots) in the Body of Christ. Without them, the churches would most likely have died.

1 John's theme:
You've lost that lovin' feeling

1 John

Writer	John
Date written	AD 85
Place written	Ephesus
Recipients	Christians in Asia Minor
Theme	You've lost that lovin' feeling

God is love, and all who live in love live in God, and God lives in them.
—1 John 4:16

During the last 30 years of his life, John made his home in Ephesus where he ministered to a circle of churches in Asia Minor. He had left Palestine some time in the mid-AD 60's, when Roman armies laid siege to Jerusalem, destroyed the city and scattered its inhabitants.

Near the end of the first century, Gnosticism, a pagan philosophy of life, gained popularity in John's part of the world. The Gnostics held a strange notion that matter, the stuff of all physical things, was inherently evil and that only spiritual things were good. As their adherents consciously infiltrated the Christian churches to recruit followers, this particular belief took on this form: Jesus only *seemed* to be human; he really wasn't—he was only a ghost.

The Gnostics also taught that the pathway to salvation lay in the pursuit of mystical, special and secret knowledge and that only their initiated cult members had access to it. To them, head knowledge was everything.

These teachings confused the believers and turned them from their hearts to their heads. And as thinking replaced communing with God, their once fervent love for Christ grew cold. Realizing the severity of the situation, John wrote this letter to declare that Jesus was a real man. As his closest disciple, John had seen, heard and traveled with Jesus for three years. And to downplay the value of mere head knowledge, John redefined the term. "We know," he said 13 times in this letter, speaking of the assurances that can only be gained through personal (heart) experiences of Christ.

Then, John redirected the faithful towards God's love, urged them to regain that warm, captivating, fulfilling, lovin' feeling they had lost and commanded them to abide there… forever.

A brief outline of the letter

1 John can be divided into three parts, each featuring one of God's divine characteristics. In the first part, God is light—in him is no darkness at all. In his light, we find forgiveness and fellowship. In the second part, real Christians express their love towards God, other believers and other people and not towards sin, the world and themselves. In the third part, eternal life can be found only in Jesus, God's Son.

	Chapters
God is light—versus the darkness of Satan and sin	1-2
God is love—expressed in loving others	3-4
God is life—eternal life, only found in the Son	5

God is light   God is love   God is life

Verses that display God's love

John reminds the believers that loving God and having a close relationship with him are the best ways to negate the damaging effects of the cults. To make his point, he uses the Greek word *agape* (God's love) 42 times.

See how very much our Father loves us, for he calls us his children. **1 John 3:1**

This is the message you have heard from the beginning: We should love one another. **3:11**

We know what real love is because Jesus gave up his life for us. **3:16**

Let's not merely say that we love each other; let us show the truth by our actions. **3:18**

Let us continue to love one another, for love comes from God. **4:7**

Anyone who does not love does not know God, for God is love. **4:8**

This is real love—not that we loved God, but that he loved us. **4:10**

Since God loved us that much, we surely ought to love each other. **4:11**

If we love each other, God lives in us, and his love is brought to full expression in us. **4:12**

God is love, and all who live in love live in God, and God lives in them. **4:16**

Such love has no fear, because perfect love expels all fear. **4:18**

Loving God means keeping his commandments. **5:3**

How to navigate 1 John

1. **Look for John's tests (PET scans)**

   "Dear friends, do not believe everyone who claims to speak by the Spirit. You must test them to see if the spirit that they have comes from God."

   1 John 4:1

   Here are the tests. According to John, real believers:

   Are transparent, hide nothing and practice the truth. **1 John 1:6**

   Freely admit that they are sinners (saved by grace). **1:8**

   Confess their sins to God and receive forgiveness. **1:10**

   Know Jesus intimately and keep his commandments. **2:3-4**

   Abide in Christ continually and live their lives as he did. **2:6**

   Love their Christian brothers and sisters. **2:10-11**

   Don't habitually love the world or worldly things. **2:15-16**

   Do righteous deeds. **3:10**

   Confess that Jesus Christ has come in the flesh. **4:1-4**

2. **Understand John's reasons for writing this letter**

   John's letter both encourages and warns the believers. He lets his readers know why he is writing to them at least five different times. Watch for them. Here they are:

   We want you to have fellowship with us (and not the bad guys). **1:3**

   We want your joy to be filled to overflowing. **1:4**

   We want to help you avoid sin. **2:1**

   We want you to know that you have eternal life. **5:13**

   We want you to continue to believe in the Son of God. **5:13**

3. **Notice the black and white**

   John uses stark contrasts to make his points clear. Here are a few of them: light and darkness / truth and lies / love and hate / Christ and Antichrist / Children of God and children of the devil / the Father and the world.

Unique things about 1 John

Did you know...

The Antichrist is coming

In 2 Thessalonians 2:3, we meet "the man of lawlessness," a real person who will come at the end times "to do the work of Satan," to oppose and replace Christ as Lord. Here, in this letter (and only here), John gives this person a name: the Antichrist (1 John 2:18).

John ran out of the bath house

Polycarp, one of John's disciples, told this story about an encounter John had with Cerinthus, a heretical leader of the anti-Christian movement, at the public baths in Ephesus. "Let us flee," John cried as he ran outside, "lest the building fall, since Cerinthus, the foe of the Truth, is within it!"

Jesus unties the devil's knots

Were John to have written an amplified version of this letter, in 1 John 3:8, he might have said, "But the Son of God (Jesus, our mighty Savior) came (appeared, came to earth, became a flesh and blood man) to destroy (untie, loosen, undo, dissolve, break up, annul, put an end to) the works (knots, entrapments, evil doings, fabrications) of the devil."

1 John is like a symphony

Unlike most letters, 1 John is not logically laid out in an organized fashion. It's more like a symphony whose dominant themes, like grand melodies, rise and fall; whose key messages, like beloved choruses, return over and over again; and whose warnings, like trumpet blasts, are unmistakable in their solemn clarity. Sit back and give it a listen.

Recap

- When you think of John's letters, think: PET scanners—diagnostic devices that search the Church (the Body of Christ) for evil people (hot spots).

- Remember that the theme of 1 John is love. It is a call for the believers to return to Christ, their first love, and fall in love with him all over again.

- John uses black and white contrasts to send powerful messages.

Read it!

- Read 1 John now. At a casual reading pace it will take you 13 minutes.

Self-study / Group discussion questions

- When John wrote this letter he was probably over 80 years old. He calls his readers "little children" nine times in five chapters. Why? What is he trying to communicate to them by using this term of endearment?

- To confront the complicated and confusing environment of Gnostic intellectualism, John calls the believers back to the basics, the origins of the truth, the fundamentals of the faith. Do you think this is an effective strategy? Why or why not?

- John commands the believers to "not love this world" (2:15). One of the most difficult challenges for believers is to be *in the world* but not *of the world*. Do you agree? If so, what makes this so difficult?

Insights that we can apply today

> We proclaim to you what we ourselves have seen and heard so that you may have fellowship with us. . . and fully share our joy.
>
> 1 John 1:3-4

Christianity is not a religion. It's a relationship—a two-dimensional flow of life—brought about by our belief in Jesus Christ. Vertically, we have a clear channel for a continuous flood of life-giving communication between Jesus and ourselves. And horizontally, we share Christ's overwhelming life supply with people around us, often soaking them with joy and generosity in the process. The Bible calls this phenomenon *fellowship*. We're telling you about it so you too can get completely soaked. Jump in—the water's fine.

2 John's theme:

Guess who's NOT coming to dinner?

2 John

Writer	John
Date written	AD 85
Place written	Ephesus
Recipients	Christians in Asia Minor
Theme	Guess who's NOT coming to dinner?

I say this because many deceivers have gone out into the world.

—2 John 7

Most Bible teachers believe that all three of John's letters were written about the same time and under similar circumstances. As we pick up the action in this second letter, some of the Gnostic infiltrators who John had identified in his first letter are taking their show on the road, leaving the larger churches in major metropolitan areas to prey on the more vulnerable Christian groups in the small towns and villages. These sinister-looking characters were NOT to be trusted.

In those days, it was common for evangelists to travel from place to place to bring Christ's message of hope and forgiveness to local residents. It was customary for folks to welcome these itinerants into their homes and provide them with food and shelter for the night.

But now, false teachers, wolves in sheep's clothing, began to knock on these same rural doors. Or, they simply showed up at home Bible studies, pretending to be Christians but intent on feeding the believers their "Jesus was just a ghost" poison. (If Jesus didn't shed real human blood on the cross, he couldn't take away the sins of the world.)

When John learned that these deceivers were on their way to one of his churches, he wrote this short note to warn them. "If anyone comes to your meeting," says John, "and does not teach the truth about Christ, don't invite that person into your home or give any kind of encouragement. Anyone who encourages such people becomes a partner in their evil work" (2 John 10).

John has much more to say to these believers. But he'll wait to speak with them face to face. He plans to visit soon.

How to navigate 2 John

1. **Realize that this is a warning letter**

    The purpose of this letter is simple. John wants to warn his *little children* of danger. They should watch out for impostors, "and whatever you do, keep those doors locked."

2. **Notice the role that truth plays**

    Whereas the banner over 1 John is *love*, the key word of 2 John is *truth*, the truth about who Jesus is. John mentions *truth* five times in the first four verses to help the believers stand their ground against the lies the false teachers would soon be throwing at them. Yes, God is love, but love is discerning and must be shared based on the truth.

3. **Know that 2 John is a miniature of 1 John**

    John teaches the same things in both letters. He encourages Christians to:

    > Live in the light of truth,
    >
    > Love one another,
    >
    > Be on guard against false teachers, and
    >
    > Be content to stick with the teachings of the apostles—
    >
    > and nothing else.

Unique things about 2 John

Did you know...

John wrote to a lady and her kids (?)

This letter is addressed to *the chosen lady and her children*. Who are these people? Some believe that this phrase is symbolic—that John is writing to a specific local church (a chosen lady) and its members (her children). Others feel that John might be writing to an actual woman and her Christian kids. If this is a home church, led by a mom, it might be both.

One sheet of papyrus

Why is 2 John so short? One reason is that John meant it to be a quick note, not a long letter. He planned to visit in person and say more. It's interesting that the full content of 2 John fits quite nicely on just one single sheet (6" by 8") of papyrus.

The deceivers were like cancer cells

The false teachers were often arrogant intellectuals who claimed that their teachings were superior to Christian theology. Like cancer cells, they grew out of control (pursuing mystical knowledge), and preyed on those around them (nearby cells). In verse nine, John warned the believers to watch out for these evil men who went beyond the teachings of Christ.

3 John's theme:

Memos to three Christian brothers with difficult names

3 John

Writer	John
Date written	AD 85
Place written	Ephesus
Recipient	Gaius
Theme	Memos to three Christian brothers with difficult names

Dear friend, don't let this bad example influence you. Follow only what is good. —3 John 11

Sometime after writing his second letter, John received a troubling report from one of the churches under his care. It seems that Diotrephes *(di-ot'-re-feez)*, a church leader, had been behaving badly by abusing his position, and in so doing had created havoc in his church.

Diotrephes loved being the focus of attention, and his intimidating, heavy-handed style crossed the line of acceptable leadership practice. Churches were supposed to be led by teams—not by one vocal individual.

What made matters worse, Diotrephes didn't much care for John or for members of his ministry team. He often criticized John in public, trying his best to malign him. If any of his parishioners gave hospitality to the traveling evangelists that came from John, Diotrephes threw them out of the church.

(Word on the street was that Diotrephes was a Gnostic sympathizer.)

But John didn't address this letter to Diotrephes. He sent it to Gaius *(gah'-yus)*, his good friend, who was a faithful member of that church. Gaius not only sided with John, he also loved to host the itinerant preachers that John sent. John wrote to Gaius to commend him for standing strong in the face of tyranny. He also wanted to introduce an ally.

Which brings us to Demetrius *(de-me'-tre-us)*, our third Christian brother, who may either have been the bearer of this letter, or one of John's traveling teachers, or both. All that we know about Demetrius is contained in one Bible verse (3 John 10). He was well spoken of 1) by John, 2) by the truth itself, and 3) by everyone. John seems to say, "Gaius, get to know this guy."

How to navigate 3 John

1. **Learn from Gaius**

   Gaius was a generous, hospitable, kind, loving, sincere, truthful, faithful, disciplined, God-honoring, loyal, industrious, conscientious, Bible-believing, service-oriented, spiritually-healthy man of God. Copy him.

2. **Learn from Diotrephes**

   On the other hand, Diotrephes was an arrogant, ambitious, headstrong, opinionated, proud, ego-driven, hot-tempered, malicious, Gnostic-leaning, independent-minded, John-hating church leader. Don't copy him.

3. **Learn from Demetrius**

   Demetrius was a beloved, well-regarded, truth-witnessing, Bible-loving missionary. John introduces Demetrius to Gaius as a like-minded resource. Copy him too.

Unique things about 3 John

Did you know...

3 John is John's second letter to this church

In verse 9 John says, "I wrote to the church about this, but Diotrephes...." John sent an earlier letter to this church, possibly to encourage them to welcome his missionaries. What happened to it? Was it ever read out loud in church? We don't know, but knowing Diotrephes, we can venture a guess.

3 John is the flipside of 2 John

In the 1960's, 45's (phonograph records that played on turntables at 45 revolutions per minute) dominated the music market. Each 45 had two sides. In his second letter, John warned folks not to open their homes to the bad guys. In his third letter, he played the flipside, encouraging the believers to warmly welcome the good guys (nice).

2 John and 3 John are like twin sisters

Both letters are short. Both encourage love. Both endorse *living according to the truth*. Both open with *the elder*. Both contain warnings. Both mention evil deeds. Both have traveling teachers. In both, John is happy. Both are written *with ink*. Jerome, an early church father, called them "twin sisters."

Recap

- 2 John is a letter of warning—lock out the false teachers.

- 3 John is an invitation—welcome in the true teachers.

- These two are the shortest letters in the New Testament.

Read it!

- Read 2 and 3 John now. At a casual reading pace it will take you 2 minutes to read each of them.

Self-study / Group discussion questions

- There are billions of cells in your body. Each grows, divides, dies and is replaced. Malignant cells are different. They grow and divide recklessly without concern for other cells or for the body itself. Think of all the ways that false teachers might behave like cancer cells. Now discuss these.

- One version of 2 John 10 says, "If anyone comes to your meeting and does not teach the truth about Christ, don't invite that person into your home." Imagine that you're living at John's time. You've just received this warning. Someone knocks on your door and claims to be a Christian teacher who needs a place to stay. What do you do? What do you say?

- In 3 John, Diotrephes is portrayed as a despicable character, though Bible teachers believe that he was a Christian. What might have caused him to become like this? Is it possible to help him? How?

Insights that we can apply today

Dear friend, I hope all is well with you and that you are as healthy in body as you are strong in spirit. —3 John 2

As John opens this letter, he sends his good friend what appears to be a rather standard set of good wishes. More often than not, we would gloss over this part as we hurry to get to the real meaty stuff. But when we slowly re-read what John says here, something remarkable pops out. John is praying that Gaius' health and the rest of his life circumstances would rise to the level of prosperity of his already exceptional, outstanding, superb, exemplary and prevailing spiritual life. Gaius' soul is prospering; the other parts of his life are trying to catch up. What a great place to be.

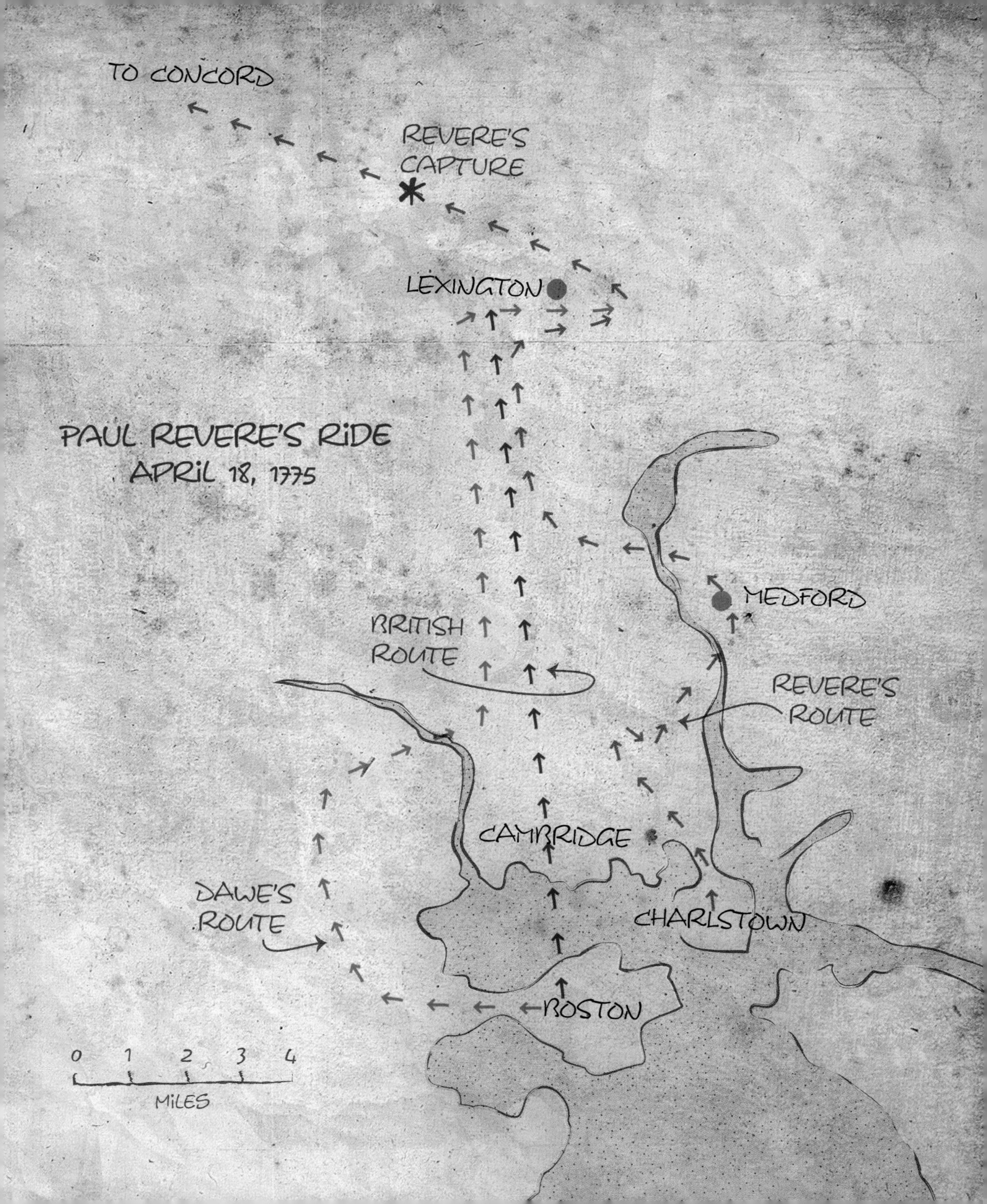

TO CONCORD

REVERE'S
CAPTURE

LEXINGTON ●

PAUL REVERE'S RIDE
APRIL 18, 1775

BRITISH
ROUTE

MEDFORD ●

REVERE'S
ROUTE

CAMBRIDGE

DAWE'S
ROUTE

CHARLSTOWN

BOSTON

0 1 2 3 4
MILES

Intro to Jude

In January 1861, a poem by Henry Wadsworth Longfellow commemorating the American Revolution appeared in the Atlantic Monthly. It opened like this:

> Listen my children and you shall hear
> Of the midnight ride of Paul Revere,
> On the 18th of April in Seventy-five;
> Hardly a man is now alive
> Who remembers that famous day and year.

This poem, "**Paul Revere's Ride**," which immortalized a midnight rider's 10-mile gallop from Charleston to Lexington, rocketed Paul Revere from virtual obscurity to folk hero status. And while Longfellow's account is largely accurate, his poem has one giant-sized omission. He failed to mention that a second rider, William Dawes, also rode to sound the alarm that night and that he left over an hour before Revere. Here's how historians believe it happened:

9:30 p.m.	*Dawes leaves Boston on horseback; rides southwest*
10:00 p.m.	*British troops prepare to cross Boston Harbor in ships*
11:00 p.m.	*Revere leaves Charlestown on horseback; rides northwest*
11:30 p.m.	*Revere "alarms almost every house" (his words) in Medford*
12:05 a.m.	*He briefs Samuel Adams and John Hancock in Lexington*
12:30 a.m.	*Dawes arrives; meets up with Revere, Adams and Hancock*
12:45 a.m.	*Revere, Dawes and a third person, Prescott, head for Concord*
1:00 a.m.	*A British patrol captures Revere; Dawes and Prescott escape*
2:00 a.m.	*Revere is freed; British troops leave Boston; march northwest*
4:00 a.m.	*Groups of patriots begin to gather in Lexington and Concord*
5:00 a.m.	*The British arrive; a shot is fired; the revolution begins*

Revere and Dawes' early warnings gave the patriots time to assemble in Lexington and Concord where they engaged the British forces. Without these two riders, the American Revolution may have unfolded quite differently.

At Jude's time, a similar covert troop movement was underway. Enemies of Christian freedom were fanning out across his region, intent on capturing believers with false teachings. Jude picked up his pen to sound the alarm.

This letter is *his* midnight ride.

Jude's theme:

Our churches have worms

Jude

Writer	Jude
Date written	AD 64
Place written	Palestine?
Recipients	Palestinian Christians
Theme	Our churches have worms

Some ungodly people have wormed their way into your churches.

—Jude 3

Jude, one of Jesus' four half-brothers, became a Christian sometime after Christ's resurrection. Like his brother James, Jude soon took on a leadership role in the early church and wrote a letter that later became part of the New Testament collection.

Apparently, Jude was living somewhere in Palestine in the late AD-60's when he decided to draft an instructional letter to the believers under his care, laying out for them the basic elements of "the salvation we all share."

As he sat down to put pen to papyrus, some troubling news crossed his desk. The group of ungodly fellows that Peter expected to arrive someday (2 Peter 2:1) had just been spotted in Jude's region worming their way into some of the churches.

Alarmed at hearing this, Jude laid aside his discipleship topic and repurposed his letter into an urgent call to arms, warning the believers to watch out for these guys. In this brief 24-verse memo, Jude went to extraordinary lengths to describe the infiltrators and their seditious activities. To encourage his readers, Jude cited Old Testament examples of similar encounters with evil people and the awful judgment God rained down on them.

With a strong sense of urgency, Jude asked the faithful to rise up, defend themselves and fight for their beliefs—in his words, "to contend earnestly for the faith which was once for all delivered to the saints" (Jude 3). With perseverance and reliance on "Him who is able to keep you from stumbling" (Jude 24), the people may have done just that.

How to navigate Jude

1. **Realize that Jude and 2 Peter are twins**

    There are many similarities between these two letters. Read Jude 4-18.
    Then read 2 Peter 2:1-18 and 3:1-4. You'll discover that these portions are
    almost identical. Either Peter borrowed from Jude's language or Jude used
    Peter's. Either way, they both vividly portrayed the same evil people.

2. **Notice that Jude's letter has two distinct parts**

    In the first part (verses 5-19), Jude uses the words *these people* repeatedly
    when he talks about the bad guys—these immoral, despicable, brute
    beasts. Then in the second part (verses 20-23), Jude switches pronouns to
    you and speaks directly to the good guys—the faithful followers of Christ—
    whom he encourages to build faith, pray and stay in God's love (cool).

3. **Discover that Jude has triplets**

    One distinguishing characteristic of Jude's writing style is his habit of
    stringing groups of three's together. Look for these triplets as you read:

vs. 1	Jude / slave of Jesus / brother of James
vs. 1	called / loves / keeps you safe
vs. 2	mercy / peace / love
vs. 4	ungodly people / turn God's grace / deny the Lord
vs. 5-7	people / angels / cities
vs. 8	live / defy / scoff
vs. 11	Cain / Balaam / Korah
vs. 16	live / brag / flatter
vs. 17	friends / apostles / Jesus
vs. 19	divisive / natural / spiritless
vs. 20-21	build / pray / await

Unique things about Jude

Did you know. . .

Jude and James wrote like brothers

Maybe that's because they *were* brothers—two of Mary and Joseph's sons and Jesus' half-brothers. Both wrote authoritatively. Both used graphic language. Neither minced words. And both created fabulous figures of speech out of their experiences of nature and the outdoors.

Clouds, trees, waves and stars

Speaking of the outdoors, in verses 12-13, Jude brings together objects from four natural spheres as metaphors for the bad guys—waterless clouds (air), dead trees (earth), wild waves (seas) and wandering stars (outer space). All four illustrate the emptiness of the false teachers' words and the hypocrisy of their lives.

Michael fought with the devil over Moses' body

According to the Old Testament, at the end of his life, Moses walked to the top of Mount Nebo, vanished from sight and died. To this day no one knows where he's buried (Deuteronomy 34:1-6). In this letter, Jude quotes a Jewish tradition that suggests that after Moses died, Michael the Archangel and Satan disputed over his body (makes us wonder why).

Recap

- Jude sounds an alarm, much like Paul Revere's midnight ride. This letter is a call to arms—to rise up and fight for the faith.

- Jude and 2 Peter are like twins: both vividly describe the same evil men.

- Jude has two sections—the bad guys and the good guys.

Read it!

- Read Jude now. At a casual reading pace it will take you 2 minutes.

Self-study / Group discussion questions

- The false teachers taught that since God freely gives grace, it's okay to live a life free of restraints. They promoted sexual pleasures as something that God supports and encourages. How would you respond if they approached you and asked you to live in this sort of freedom?

- Jude opens his letter with warm greetings and strong affirmations, giving rich blessings to his readers. He then warns them, in countless ways, to watch out for the bad guys. As he closes, he provides practical ways for the believers to reject the false teachings and maintain their Christian faith. Why does Jude structure his letter in this way?

- In verse 4, Jude says that "ungodly people have wormed their way" into the churches. What does this tell you about the motives and ethics of these people? Why did they have to be so secretive?

Insights that we can apply today

Glory to God, who is able to keep you from falling... —Jude 24

At the end of his short letter, Jude invokes a fabulous blessing on his readers,
the believers. This blessing is for you too. Read it, enjoy it, and as you do,
put your hand in God's hand.

Now to him who is able to keep you from stumbling,
And to present you faultless
Before the presence of his glory with exceeding joy,
To God our Savior,
Who alone is wise,
Be glory and majesty,
Dominion and power,
Both now and forever.
Amen.

Prophecy

Intro to Revelation

In August 1967, two Canadian filmmakers, Graeme Ferguson and Roman Kroitor, met in Montreal to kick around ideas for creating large-format films. Earlier that year, Kroitor's multi-screen film *In the Labyrinth* had become *the* runaway hit of Canada's Expo 67. A million moviegoers clamored for more.

But there was a problem. Though using multiple projectors to throw multiple images on multiple screens had worked, it was at best a clumsy way to project movies. "We asked each other," said Ferguson, "'Wouldn't it be better to have a single, large-format projector to fill a large screen?'"

That afternoon they went to work. "We talked for about an hour," said Ferguson, "and within that hour we had sketched out the screen size that could be used and the film format that would be capable of filling it." Without realizing it, they had just given birth to IMAX® (short for maximum image), the world's largest theatre projection system.

Their big ideas quickly became reality as Ferguson and Kroitor recruited technical experts to design the large-sized cameras, projectors and screens needed to support a larger film format. What they invented was enormous:

Film: a horizontal film frame that is 10 times larger than Hollywood's standard frame. If 35mm frames are stamps, an IMAX® frame is a post card.

Projector: a two-ton behemoth that sucks in film at a rate of five feet per second. A two and an half hour film is 8 miles long and weighs 700 pounds.

Projection bulb: a 15,000 watt, water-cooled, quartz-glass bulb filled with Xenon gas that burns twice as hot as the sun and is three times brighter.

Screens: as tall as 8-story buildings and wide enough to wrap beyond peripheral vision, drilled with thousands of tiny holes to project sound.

But as impressive as this is, if it's immense motion pictures you're after, check out this scene from the book of Revelation—it filled the entire sky: "Then I witnessed in heaven an event of great significance... I saw a woman clothed with the sun, with the moon beneath her feet, and a crown of twelve stars on her head." And this is only one scene. There are 59 more, waiting for you at God's Revelation Theatre, the New Testament's MEGA IMAX®.

Revelation's theme:
God's lion returns, routs and reigns

Revelation

Writer	John
Date written	AD 95
Place written	Patmos
Recipients	Seven churches in Asia
Theme	God's lion returns, routs and reigns

On his robe... was written... King of all kings and Lord of all lords.

—Revelation 19:16

Near the end of the first century, while John is serving hard time on the island of Patmos for his crime of propagating Christianity, Jesus suddenly appears to him, from out of nowhere, scaring him half to death.

"When I saw him," says John, "I fell at his feet as if I were dead." "Don't be afraid!" says Jesus (probably a wee bit too late). His snow-white hair, piercing eyes and flowing robes give him a commanding presence and make him look rather high-priestly.

"Write down what you've seen," he says, dazzling John with a scene of seven blazing lamp stands, "both the things that are now happening and the things that will happen." And over a period of time, as Jesus takes him to heaven and back, creating for him a tapestry of 60 eye-popping visions, John tries his best to put into words what he sees and hears.

The result is the book of Revelation, John's 22-chapter compilation of the visions of hope that Jesus gave him on the island. As instructed, John sends his finished manuscript to seven churches in today's Turkey to strengthen the believers during times of severe persecution.

What makes the book so hopeful is the story that its 60 connected visions tell—a story of good conquering evil, of a just God dealing forcefully with the world's injustice, of Christ, the King of all kings and Lord of all lords, returning to earth to reign forever in glory and peace.

As we look into Revelation, the last New Testament book, notice that we've come full circle from Matthew, the first New Testament book. Both show us Christ as a lion. In Matthew, he merely roars. But in Revelation, he returns, routs and reigns. Amen. Come, Lord Jesus!

A brief outline of the book

After a one-chapter introduction, chapters 2-3 contain seven letters that Jesus sent to actual churches that existed at that time. From there the action moves to the future, as chapters 4-11 present a wide-angle view of the sweep of events that occur from Christ's ascension until his coming back. These scenes unfold in an ordered sequence with a twist—John covers the same material twice. Chapters 12-20 repeat the overview John presented in chapters 4-11, this time using a close-up lens. The book then ends with spectacular scenes of eternity in chapters 21 and 22.

	Chapters
Intro—John on the island, Jesus appears	1
Letters—Jesus dictates seven letters to seven churches	2-3
Now and later—(overview)—a wide-angle view of the end times	4-11
Now and later—(details)—close-ups of the same events	12-20
Later—a new heaven, a new earth and New Jerusalem	21-22

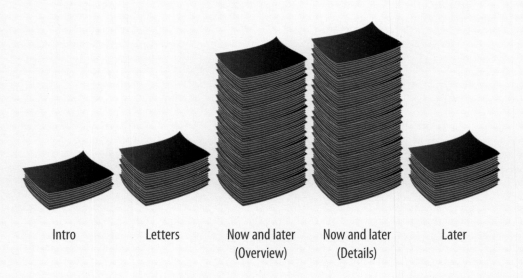

Intro   Letters   Now and later   Now and later   Later
                            (Overview)   (Details)

Verses that uniquely reveal Jesus Christ

"The Revelation of Jesus Christ," the opening phrase of this book in most translations, conveys two meanings. On one hand, it speaks of the revelation given **from** Jesus Christ to John. On the other, it means the unveiling **of** Jesus Christ for, in this book, Jesus is revealed in unique and special ways found nowhere else in the Bible. Here are a few of them:

Jesus Christ. He is the faithful witness… the first to rise from the dead, and the ruler of all the kings of the earth. **Revelation 1:5a**

Him who loves us and has freed us from our sins by shedding his blood for us. **1:5b**

"I am the First and the Last." **1:17**

"I am the living one. I died, but look—I am alive forever and ever!" **1:16**

The one who is holy and true. The one who has the key of David. **3:7**

The Amen—the faithful and true witness, the beginning of God's new creation. **3:14**

The Lion of the tribe of Judah, the heir to David's throne. **5:5**

The Lamb who was slaughtered. **5:12**

A white horse was standing there. Its rider was named Faithful and True. **19:11**

And his title was the Word of God. **19:13**

On his robe… was written this title: King of all kings and Lord of all lords. **19:16**

"I, Jesus… am both the source of David and heir to his throne. I am the bright morning star." **22:16**

How to navigate Revelation

1. **Be aware of the book's four themes**

   Four major activities take place in Revelation: 1) God judges,
   2) Christ returns, 3) God's kingdom comes and 4) eternity is unveiled.
   Look for them.

2. **Understand the flow of the story**

   In this book, God clears away the negatives before he introduces the
   positives. First, he eliminates the evils of this present world by destroying
   Satan and his followers. Then, he establishes a kingdom and prepares a
   new heaven, a new earth and a new city for Christ's followers.

3. **Keep God's judgments straight**

   Starting in chapter six, God's judgments on evil, sinful and corrupted
   things are triggered by a series of three symbolic events: 1) the opening of
   the seals of a scroll, 2) the sounding of trumpets and 3) the pouring out of
   the contents of bowls. To help you keep track of what's happening, Bible
   teachers have proposed the following sequential and nested structure:

4. **Read to see Jesus**

   With so much symbolism filling the pages of this wonderful book, it's often
   difficult to understand everything you read. Don't worry. This is a normal
   experience. For the time being, park your questions in a safe place and
   read on, allowing God's Word to feed you. You will be blessed if you do.

Unique things about Revelation

Did you know. . .

6+1=7

Numbers, in the Bible, often convey symbolic meanings. The number 1, for instance, suggests uniqueness and often pertains to God. And since man was created on the sixth day, 6 is the number of human beings. Add God to people (6+1) and you get completeness, symbolized by 7, a number that appears over 50 times in Revelation, the book of the completion of God's purpose. Man without God (6+0) is empty, alone, incomplete. This is why Antichrist, the consummate godless person, is numbered 666.

Both John and Paul wrote to 7 places

In Revelation 1:11, Jesus asked John to send letters to churches in seven cities—Ephesus, Smyrna, Pergamos, Thyatira, Sardis, Philadelphia and Laodicea. Paul's letters were also sent to seven places—Rome, Corinth, Galatia, Ephesus, Philippi, Colossae and Thessalonica (hmm... a coincidence?).

To the victors go the rewards

Seven times in Revelation chapters 2 and 3 the Lord Jesus encourages his followers to be "overcomers," those who maintain their faithfulness to him in spite of persecution or life's challenges. Christ promises special rewards for these victors, redeemable when they see him face to face.

The bad guys mimic the good guys

Our God is a Trinity—Father, Son, Spirit. In this book, which consummates the struggle between good and evil, it is a satanic trinity that fights against God. Satan, who has always wanted to be like God, opposes the Father. The Antichrist (the beast, Revelation 13:1) impersonates Christ. The false prophet (Revelation 19:20) mimics the Holy Spirit. In the end, the good guys win (and win BIG).

Recap

- To read the book of Revelation is to watch spectacular motion pictures.

- The New Testament opens with Jesus, God's lion, roaring. The New Testament ends with this same lion routing and reigning.

- It's okay if you can't figure out everything you read. For now, it's fine to read the book primarily for the vision of Jesus that it gives.

Read it!

- Read Revelation now. At a casual reading pace, it will take you one hour. You can finish it in three 20-minute sessions.

Self-study / Group discussion questions

- In this book, God uses symbolic language to convey meaning. What are the potential advantages of this type of presentation for John's readers? For today's readers? What are the potential disadvantages?

- Turn to the verses on page 347 that provide unique descriptions of Christ. Which titles impress you the most? What are your top three? Why?

- Revelation 22:20 contains the shortest prayer in the Bible, "Come, Lord Jesus." Why is this the most important prayer in the Bible?

Insights that we can apply today

Look! I stand at the door and knock. If you hear my voice and open the door, I will come in, and we will share a meal together as friends.

—Revelation 3:20

This verse pictures Jesus standing outside, knocking loudly so that we will open up and let him come inside. We often think that we are the ones who initiate contact with God. Yet in truth, he is the one who relentlessly pursues us, bringing spiritual nourishment with him. We just have to stop long enough to hear him, open the door and invite him in. Why not do this right now?

Afterwords

Congratulations. You made it to the end of your tour. You now have the **frameworks** you need to guide your Bible reading and to better understand its context. Keep them handy. Refer to them often. Use them to build your Bible skills and to bolster your confidence. Familiarity breeds empowerment. May these simple constructs make the Bible more accessible, meaningful and enjoyable to you, wherever life may take you. Have a great trip.

Notes

PART ONE

21 **Galilee...about two million people lived here:** William Smith, *Smith's Bible Dictionary* (Nashville: Thomas Nelson), 203.

21 **Perea...whose name appears nowhere in the Bible:** Merrill C. Tenney, *The Zondervan Pictoral Bible Dictionary* (Grand Rapids, MI: Zondervan, 1964), 635.

22 **think of Jesus' life in seven distinct phases:** The idea of breaking down Jesus' life and ministry into distinct, manageable chunks came from A.T. Robertson's *A Harmony of the Gospels for Students of the Life of Christ* (New York: Harper & Row, 1922).

25 **he and his dad are probably also stonemasons:** The Greek word for carpenter is *tekton*, a word "used of any artisan or craftsman in metal, or in stone as well as in wood and even of sculpture. It is certain that Jesus worked in wood...He may also have worked in stone and may even have helped build stone synagogues in Galilee like that in Capernaum." A.T. Robertson, *Word Pictures in the New Testament,* Volume 1 (Nashville: Broadman Press, 1930), 306.

25 **Sepphoris, a Greek city:** "The Surprises of Sepphoris," Frontline, PBS. http://www.pbs.org/wgbh/pages/frontline/shows/religion/jesus/sepphoris.html

33 **shouting, "Hosanna, Hosanna" at the top of their lungs:** A.T. Robertson, *Word Pictures,* Volume 1, 167.

40 **the third Council of Carthage:** David F. Payne, "The Text and Canon of the New Testament," *The International Bible Commentary* (Grand Rapids, MI: Zondervan, 1986), 1007.

41 **Stephen Langton:** "Community Jeopardy (1 Corinthians 10:14-11:1)," http://bible.org/search/apachesolr_search/Stephan%20Langton

41 **Robert Stephanus:** "How and when the Bible divided into chapters and verses," http://bible.org/question/how-and-when-was-bible-divided-chapters-and-verses

45   **John's mom, Salome:** In his Gospel, Mark identifies Salome as one of the women who stood at the cross during Jesus' crucifixion. Matthew calls this same person "the mother of Zebedee's (John's father's) sons," while John refers to her as Jesus' "mother's sister" (Jesus' aunt). Alfred Edersheim, *The Life and Times of Jesus of Nazareth,* Volume 2 (New York: Longmans, Green, 1912), 602-603; J.H. Bernard, *Gospel According to St. John: The International Critical Commentary,* Volume 2 (Edinburgh: T&T Clark, 1963), 631.

44   **Luke...May have been a blood brother of Titus:** Early on, both Luke and Titus were connected with the city of Antioch. Merrill C. Tenney, *New Testament Survey* (Grand Rapids, MI: Eerdman's, 1961), 142.

54   **Theme—What is this book about?:** The theme phrase for each book has intentionally been designed to stick in readers' minds. For a fascinating discussion of how to create sticky ideas see: Chip Heath & Dan Heath, *Made to Stick: Why Some Ideas Survive and Others Die* (New York: Random House, 2008), 285-289.

PART TWO
Biographies of Christ

63   **"the most important book in the world":** This description of the Gospel of Matthew came from Ernest Renan, a French historian, philosopher and religious scholar during the mid-1800's. Sherman E. Johnson, *The Gospel According to St. Matthew: The Interpreter's Bible* (Nashville: Abington Press, 1951), 232.

67   **Matthew referenced the Old Testament over 90 times:** Homer A. Kent, *The Gospel According to Matthew: The Wycliffe Bible Commentary* (Chicago: Moody Press, 1962), 929.

71   **Tax collectors obsess on money:** John F. Walvoord and Roy B. Zuck, *The Bible Knowledge Commentary,* New Testament Edition (Wheaton, IL: Victor Books, 1984), 15.

75 **Mark was dwarfed in his shadow:** Donald Guthrie strikes a vivid contrast between a "neglected" Mark and a "stately" Matthew in his comprehensive: *New Testament Introduction* (Downers Grove, IL: InterVarsity Press, 1970), 53-54.

75 **But then one day in 1863:** The fascinating story of Holtzman's role in Mark's rise from rags to riches is told by Walter Wessel in his introduction to Mark in: *The Expositor's Bible Commentary,* Volume 8 (Grand Rapids, MI: Zondervan, 1984), 603-605.

77 **"There was no animal":** William Smith, *Dictionary,* 471.

78 **According to tradition:** Many Bible scholars believe that Peter was the source of Mark's writing. Frederic Godet provides the account that appears here in his classic: *Introduction to the New Testament* (Edinburgh: T&T Clark, 1899), 22-24.

82 **Experience Mark's run-ons first-hand:** There are 66 *ands* in Mark chapter three. Bible teacher J. Vernon McGee says that *and* occurs 1,331 times in Mark's book: *Thru the Bible with J. Vernon McGee,* Volume 4 (Pasadena, CA: Thru the Bible Radio, 1983), 158.

83 **Call me Stump-fingers:** Wessel, *Expositor's*, 606. Mark is said to have had "short fingers in comparison with the size of the rest of his body."

83 **A naked teenager runs away:** Darrell L. Bock, *The Gospel of Mark: Cornerstone Biblical Commentary,* Volume 11 (Carol Stream, IL: Tyndale House, 2005), 536.

87 **Luke the Painter:** Much has been written of the legend that Luke was a painter. William Barclay speaks to it briefly in his *The Gospel of Luke* (Philadelphia: Westminster Press, 1956), vii. According to Catholic sources, Luke is the Patron Saint of 20 different crafts and professions. See http://saints.sqpn.com/saint-luke-the-evangelist and www.catholic.org/saints

87 **"The most beautiful book ever written":** Merrill F. Unger, *The New Unger's Bible Dictionary* (Chicago: Moody Press, 1988).

89 **"The Greeks attempted":** McGee, *Thru the Bible, 239.*

89 **"Whereas the emphasis":** Sidlow Baxter, *Explore the Book,* Volume 5 (Grand Rapids, MI: Zondervan, 1962), 232.

91 **Luke was a Greek Christian missionary and pastor:** Bible scholar Frederic Godet believes that after Paul, Silas and Timothy left Philippi shortly after establishing the first church in Europe there (Acts 16:40), Luke stayed behind, remaining attached to (pastoring) the church for a number of years. *A Commentary on the Gospel of St. Luke,* (New York: I.K. Funk, 1881), 12.

91 **"This prologue precisely resembles":** Frederic Godet, *Studies on the New Testament* (London: Hodder and Stoughton, 1880), 41.

99 **"Eating a hearty bowl":** adapted from "Origins of First 'Restaurant' Challenged after 200 Years," an article by Julian Coman in *The Telegraph* (London, England), September 3, 2000.

99 **"For many Christians":** William Barclay, *The Gospel of John,* Volume 1 (Philadelphia: Westminster Press, 1956), xv.

101 **"the eagles' wings are figurative":** C.F. Keil and F. Delitzsch, *Commentary on the Old Testament,* Volume 1 (Grand Rapids, MI: Eerdmans, 1980), 96.

101 **"He is unparalleled":** Anne Graham Lotz, *Just Give Me Jesus* (Nashville: Word Publishing, 2000), 1.

103 **So one day, they approached John:** Philip W. Comfort and Wendel C. Hawley, *Opening John's Gospel and Epistles* (Carol Stream, IL: Tyndale House, 2007), 5.

History

113 **Richard C. Rothermel:** Gail Wells, "The Rothermel Fire-Spread Model: Still Running Like a Champ," *Fire Science Digest,* Issue 2, (March 2008); A. Long, D. Kennard, "Rate of Spread," *Forest Encyclopedia Network,* USDA Forest Service, November 14, 2008, 478; http://www.forestencyclopedia. net/p/p478

115 **"Through the Spirit":** N.T. Wright, *Acts for Everyone,* Part One (Louisville: Westminster JKP, 2008), 22, 25.

116 **the Way...had developed quite a bad reputation:** William J. Larkin, *Acts: Cornerstone Biblical Commentary,* Volume 12 (Carol Stream, IL: Tyndale House, 2006), 253-257.

121 **"The most perfect account":** R.H.C. Lenski, *The Interpretation of the Acts of the Apostles* (Minneapolis: Ausburgh, 1961), 6.

125 **Barnabas is Mark's uncle:** Donald Guthrie, *NT Introduction,* 71.

129 **This amazing edifice:** "Temple of Artemis." *Encyclopedia Britannica Online.* http://www.britannica.com/EBchecked/topic/36816/Temple-of-Artemis.

133 **he has his day in court:** Most Bible scholars support the hypothesis that Paul had two Roman imprisonments, separated by a period of freedom. Among them is Robert H. Gundry: *A Survey of the New Testament,* Third Edition (Grand Rapids, MI: Zondervan, 1994), 412.

133 **he is sent to his heavenly rest:** John Pollock, *The Apostle: A Life of Paul* (Colorado Springs, CO: Cook Communications, 1985), 307-308.

Paul's letters to churches

136 **First century letter writing:** Calvin J. Roetzel, *The Letters of Paul: Conversations in Context,* Fourth Edition (Louisville: Westminster JKP), 51-55. Roetzel's chart appears on **frameworks** page 137.

139 **Fortuna:** Lawrence Richardson, *A New Topical Dictionary of Ancient Rome* (Baltimore, MD: Johns Hopkins, 1992), 229; Susanne William Rasmussen, *Public Portents in Republican Rome* (Rome, Italy: L'Erma di Bretschneider, 2003), 68.

143 **During a trip to Corinth:** Griffith Thomas, *St. Paul's Epistle to the Romans* (Grand Rapids, MI: Eerdmans, 1956), 16-22.

147 **Benedictions, benedictions, benedictions:** A. Berkeley Mickelsen, *Romans: The Wycliffe Bible Commentary* (Chicago: Moody Press, 1962), 1180.

147 **Phoebe is the first female deacon:** William Sanday, *The Epistle to the Romans: The International Critical Commentary* (New York: Scribners, 1896), 416-418.

151 **the perfect storm:** The name given by the National Weather Service to the October 30, 1991 storm off the Eastern Seaboard of the United States. This storm was the basis for Sebastian Junger's best-selling book of the same name. "The Perfect Storm," NOAA Satellite and Information Service. http://www.ncdc.noaa.gov/oa/satellite/satelliteseye/cyclones/ pfctstorm91/pfctstorm.html

153 **"The famous commercial prosperity":** Donald Guthrie, *The New Bible Commentary: Revised* (Grand Rapids, MI: Eerdmans, 1978), 1049.

153 **no one could walk along any street:** Frederic Godet, *Studies in Paul's Epistles* (Grand Rapids, MI: Kregel, 1984), 70.

153 **"In an atmosphere of moral laxity":** Guthrie, *New Testament Introduction,* 421-422.

154 **"The Church in Corinth":** Godet, *Studies in Paul's Epistles,* 67.

157 **"The church at Corinth was a vexing problem":** Tenney, *New Testament Survey,* 294.

159 **Paul made tents for a living:** From a lecture given by Costas Tsevas, Biblical Tour Guide and Scholar of Ancient Greek History and Languages at the museum, Corinth, Greece on September 25, 2008.

163 **Dr. Howard Florey:** This story appeared in the October 3, 2005 issue of Science Watch, an online subscription service that reports on significant science. Norman Healey, who was interviewed for the article, "Making Penicillin Possible: Norman Healey Remembers," was a research colleague of Dr. Florey at Oxford University in the 1940's. http://archive.sciencewatch.com/interviews/norman_heatly.htm

166 **Paul's letters and visits:** Donald Guthrie does a masterful job (as always) in recreating Paul's multiple visits (and letters) to Corinth. Guthrie, *New Testament Introduction,* 424-439.

170 **"The human Paul is very much in evidence":** Tenney, *New Testament Survey,* 300.

171 **Paul took a secret trip to heaven:** "The first heaven is that of the clouds, the air; the second, that of the stars, the sky: the third is spiritual." Robert Jamieson, A.R. Fausset and David Brown, *Commentary Critical and Explanatory on the Whole Bible,* Volume 2 (New York: Scranton, 1875), 319.

171 **Paul had a thorn in the flesh:** Though the Bible doesn't say what Paul's "thorn in the flesh" was, most Bible scholars believe that Paul was speaking here of some sort of physical infirmity. Suggested afflictions include migraines, earaches, malaria, epilepsy or stammering speech. That Galatians 4:15 says that the believers would have "taken out their own

eyes and given them to me (Paul)" might also suggest eye disease. W.J. Conybeare and J.S. Howson, *The Life and Epistles of St Paul,* Volume 2 (New York: Charles Scribner, 1885), 145.

175 **"liberté egalité, fraternité":** "French Revolution," Encyclopedia Britannica. http://www.britannica.com/EBchecked/topic/219315/French-Revolution

181 **the Emancipation Proclamation:** Max Lucado, *Life Lessons with Max Lucado—Book of Galatians* (Nashville: Thomas Nelson, 2007), vii.

185 **Mona Lisa:** Alan Riding, "In Louvre, New Room With View of 'Mona Lisa,'" *New York Times,* April 6, 2005.

185 **Says Vasari, "This work…":** "…the myth of Mona Lisa," *Treasures of the World,* PBS.org. http://www.pbs.org/treasuresoftheworld/a_nav/mona_nav/mnav_level_1/4myth_monafrm.html

185 **"Today's art critics":** "…Leonardo's masterful techinque," *Treasures of the World,* PBS.org. http://www.pbs.org/treasuresoftheworld/a_nav/mona_nav/mnav_level_1/3technique_monafrm.html

185 **"Among the Epistles bearing the name of St. Paul":** S.D.F. Salmond, *The Expositor's Greek Testament:* Volume 3 (Grand Rapids, MI: Eerdmans, 1960), 208.

187 **This one will be a *circular letter*:** Harold W. Hoehner, *Ephesians: Cornerstone Biblical Commentary,* Volume 16 (Carol Stream, IL: Tyndale House, 2008), 15-16.

191 **Christians are God's poem:** Hoerner, *Cornerstone,* Volume 16, 52.

195 **"You are about to embark upon a great crusade":** You can read the full transcript (or hear the actual audio) of General Eisenhower's message sent to the Allied troops just prior to the D-Day invasion at the U.S. Army's website. http://www.army.mil/d-day/message.html

195 **"I am deeply grateful for your fine message":** In an email that was received from Mary Burtzloff, Archivist at the Dwight D. Eisenhower Library in Abilene, Kansas on April 26, 2011, Mary quotes from an undated draft of a thank you letter sent from Eisenhower to De Gaulle.

197 **Some say it's because…:** Baxter, *Explore the Book,* Volume 6, 181.

198 **A letter written by a traveling father:** Tenney, *Survey,* 678.

200 **Study the "Christ Hymn":** Bible scholar Philip Comfort creates a more poetic rendering of Paul's "poem" in his Commentary on Philippians: Philip W. Comfort, *Philippians: Cornerstone Biblical Commentary,* Volume 16 (Carol Stream, IL: Tyndale House, 2008), 172.

201 **Caesar's bodyguards and household...:** It boggles the mind to realize that when Paul was imprisoned in Rome, there was a "large body of Christians in the Imperial household." You might think that Caesar's Palace would be the last place on earth to find Christians. Can you visualize Bible studies there? See H.A.A. Kennedy, *The Expositor's Greek Testament:* Volume 3 (Grand Rapids, MI: Eerdmans, 1960), 404-405. Further, it seems that some of these Palace Christians may have been soldiers who had friends in the Roman garrison at Philippi. This may be why Paul sent special greetings to these Philippians from "God's people... in Caesar's household" (Phil 4:22).

205 **That's when two architects:** The race to build the tallest building on earth is brilliantly told by: Neal Bascomb, *Higher: A Historic Race to the Sky and the Making of a City* (New York: Doubleday, 2003).

207 **Epaphras is a friend of Paul's:** This commonly-held story, paraphrased here, is recounted in many Colossian Commentaries. Among them: Godet, *Studies in Paul's Epistles,* 163-172.

210 **Understand the strange brew:** Gundry, *Survey,* 394-395.

211 **Christ *spoils* his foes:** From a lecture given by Costas Tsevas in Corinth, Greece, September 25, 2008.

215 **Leonidas:** Costas Tsevas, a lecture on the Battle of Thermopylae, September 24, 2008.

221 **Christians will be abducted:** Greek scholar Kenneth Wuest explains the literal meaning of the term "caught up" (1 Thess 4:17) in Warren Wiersbe's commentary: Warren W. Wiersbe, *The Wiersbe Bible Commentary:* New Testament (Colorado Springs, CO: David C. Cook, 2007), 721-722.

221 **a string of glittering diamonds:** S.W. Green, *Hastings Dictionary of the Bible* (Peabody, MA: Hendrickson Publishers, 2001), 930.

229 **There are no Old Testament quotes (at all):** Jamieson, Faucett and Brown, *Commentary,* Volume 2, 384.

Paul's letters to people

235 **Speaking of legendary coaches:** Mike Puma provides highlights of Wooden's life in: "Wooden ended a winner," ESPN Classic, July 5, 2005. http://espn.go.com/classic/s/add_wooden_john.html

235 **"I never had a player I didn't love":** Quotes from John Wooden are taken from: John Wooden and Jay Carty, *Coach Wooden's Pyramid of Success Playbook* (Ventura, CA: Regal Books, 2005) and from http://www.achievement.org/autodoc/page/woo0int-1

241 **Paul sings the *incarnation hymn*:** Philip H. Towner, *1-2 Timothy & Titus: The IVP New Testament Commentary Series* (Downers Grove, IL: InterVarsity Press, 1994), 96-100.

241 **We've got dancing dolphins:** According to Costas Tsevas, in 1 Tim 3:15, the word "behave" in the original Greek *(anastrethesmai)* is a word that describes the beautiful back and forth movements of dolphins in the water.

245 **The world's first compass...a *south pointer*:** In the Spring of 1997, as a part of the History of Science and Technology Program at Smith College in Northampton, MA, students created models of the ancient inventions they were studying. One of these inventions was the first compass, a *south pointer*, pictured by the model on **frameworks** page 244. You can see all of the models that were created by students at the Smith Museum website. An article by Susan Silverman describing the south pointer can be found at http://www.smith.edu/hsc/museum/ancient_inventions/compass2.html

245 **"When the people of Zheng go out to collect jade":** Joseph Needham and Colin A. Roman, *The Shorter Science and Civilisation in China* (Cambridge, Great Britain: Cambridge University Press, 1986), 23.

247 **Paul too is swept up in this crackdown:** Tenney, *Survey,* 338-339.

251 **Famous people visited Paul in jail:** W.J. Conybeare and J.S. Howson, *The Life and Epistles of St Paul,* Volume 2 (New York: Charles Scribner, 1855), 474.

251 **A coat, books and parchments:** Gundry, *Survey,* 417; and Pollock, *The Apostle,* 303.

251 **The victor's wreath:** From a lecture by Costas Tsevas at King Philips' Tomb in Vergina, Greece, September 23, 2008.

255 **"The Devil's cigarette lighter":** From the Texas Historical Assn. online: http://www.tshaonline.org/handbook/online/articles/fad29. Also a spectacular 3-minute video of Red and his team putting out this fire (from the History Channel) can be seen at: http://www.metacafe.com/watch/231727/the_devils_cigarette_lighter/

257 **Titus' conversion was so impressive:** Tenney, *Survey,* 336-337.

257 **"Other attempts at reconciliation":** Philip Comfort and Walter A. Elwell, *The Complete Book of Who's Who in the Bible* (Carol Stream, IL: Tyndale House, 2004), 584.

257 **His remarkable success earned him:** Towner, *1-2 Timothy & Titus,* 221.

260 **he might be Luke (the writer's) brother:** Tenney, *Survey,* 274.

261 **"The people of Crete are all liars":** A.T. Robertson, *Word Pictures,* Volume 4, 600.

261 **"This is a trustworthy saying":** Charles F. Pfeiffer and Everett F. Harrison, *The Epistle to Titus: The Wycliffe Bible Commentary* (Chicago: Moody Press, 1962), 1396.

261 **Lies, lies and no lies:** In Titus 1:2, Paul's short phrase, "God—who does not lie" takes on added significance against the backdrop of typical Cretan (lying) behavior: Marvin R. Vincent, *Word Studies in the New Testament,* Volume 4 (Grand Rapids, MI: Eerdmans, 1969), 337.

263 **"This word hope means different things":** Towner, *1-2 Timothy & Titus,* 219.

265 **Ben Hur®:** Copyright Warner Bros. Entertainment, Inc.

265 **"slaves were not legally considered persons":** John MacArthur, *The MacArthur Study Bible* (Nashville: Thomas Nelson, 1997), 1890-1891.

269 **Philemon is a family affair:** Godet, *Studies in Paul's Epistles,* 215-216.

269 **Many Roman slaves were highly educated:** Marvin R. Vincent, *Epistles to the Philippians and to Philemon: The International Critical Commentary* (New York: Charles Scribner, 1895), 162-163.

General letters

275 **"Southern Wisconsin is a hotbed for Tug of War:** From an interview with Shelby Richardson on August 26, 2011.

275 **Athletic contests between two teams:** Lorraine Best, "Oregon Tuggers pulling for gold at World Games in South Africa," *The Oregon Observer,* August 26, 2011; and "History of Tug of War," *TWIF Rules Manual Edition 2011* (Orfordville, WI: Tug of War Int'l Federation), 5-6. http://www.tugofwar-twif.org/?p=organisation&id=23&nav=0

277 **the Tabernacle, a large mobile worship center:** It's interesting to realize that whereas the Ten Commandments are given in 15 verses in the book of Exodus, the Tabernacle, the greatest symbol of Jesus Christ in the Bible, spans 15 chapters. In one Bay Area Bible study group, we spent 40 weeks studying the symbolism of the Tabernacle (complete with a scale model) and we still didn't cover everything. See A.B. Simpson, *Christ in the Tabernacle* (Camp Hill, PA: Wing Spread, 2009).

281 **The Christian life is like riding a bicycle:** Henrietta Mears, *What the Bible is All About* (Grand Rapids, MI: Family Christian Press, 2001), 592.

285 **"Helen was lying on the floor":** Anne's own words, from her private letters: Helen Keller, Anne Sullivan, et.al., *The Story of My Life: Restored Classic* (W.W. Norton, 2003). Quotes were taken from http://www.ralphmag.org/CB/helen-keller.html

287 **There are four different James' mentioned:** MacArthur, *Bible,* 1924.

289 **In this five-chapter letter... 54 take action verbs:** Walvoord and Zuck, *Bible Knowledge Commentary,* 816.

291 **The demons are freaking out:** The Greek word for "tremble in terror" in James 2:19 is *phrisso.* "The meaning of this Greek word in today's English," says Costas Tsevas in a lecture on September 19, 2011, "is to completely freak out. The demons are doomed, and they know it."

291 **James had camels' knees:** T. Carson, *James: The International Bible Commentary* (Grand Rapids, MI: Zondervan, 1986), 1534.

295 **"It is quite simply breathtaking":** This 6-minute video tells Sharon Chart's story and shows her in action. www.youtube.com/watch?v=q6QjZ9TGvK0

301 **Angels are curious little rascals:** John Calvin, *Calvin's Commentaries: Commentaries on the Catholic Epistles* (Grand Rapids, MI: Baker, 2009), 42-43. See also Vincent, *Word Studies,* Volume 1, 635. Charles Wesley's great hymn, "And Can It Be That I Should Gain," speaks of angel curiosity in its second verse: *"'Tis mystery all! Th' Immortal dies! Who can explore His strange design? In vain the firstborn seraph tries to sound the depths of love divine! 'Tis mercy all! Let earth adore, let angel minds inquire no more."*

301 **Jesus visited the underworld:** Gundry, *Survey,* 441-442.

309 **"Grace, not judgment, is the leading note of God's music":** Gerrit Verkuyl, *The Holy Bible, The Berkeley Version in Modern English: New Testament* (Grand Rapids, MI: Zondervan, 1960), 261.

313 **"About midway through (Jennifer's) pregnancy":** Martle Callaghan, "Metro Region PET Center and Woodburn Nuclear Medicine: The Marvel of PET Technology," *D.C. Metro M.D. News* (Sunshine Media, 2008). http://www.metroregionpet.com/mdnews.pdf

314 **You've lost that lovin' feeling:** The name of the 1964 hit song by Bill Medley and Bobby Hatfield (a.k.a, the Righteous Brothers) that stands as the most-played song in the history of American radio. http://65.175.91.44/righteousbrothers/bio.htm

319 **John ran out of the bath house:** David Smith, *The Expositor's Greek Testament,* Volume 5 (Grand Rapids, MI: Eerdmans), 157.

319 **1 John is like a symphony:** Tenney, *Survey,* 378.

325 **One sheet of papyrus:** Philip W. Comfort and Wendell C. Hawley, *1-3 John: The Cornerstone Biblical Commentary,* Volume 13 (Carol Stream, IL: Tyndale House, 2007), 383.

329 **2 John and 3 John are like twin sisters:** Hastings, *Dictionary,* 486.

333 **Paul Revere's Ride:** "The Real Story of Revere's Ride," The Paul Revere House. http://www.paulreverehouse.org/ride/real.html

333 **Revere "alarms almost every house":** "Letter from Paul Revere to Jeremy Belknap, circa 1798," The Massachusetts Historical Society. http://www.masshist.org/database/doc-viewer.php?item_id=99

337 **Michael fought with the devil over Moses' body:** Vincent, *Word Studies: Volume 1,* 715-716.

Prophecy

343 **"We asked each other," said Ferguson:** Wyndham Wise, "The Man Who Invented IMAX: An Interview with Graeme Ferguson csc" (Canadian Society of Cinematographers, December 2010). http://www.csc.ca/news/default.asp?aID=1464

348 **Keep God's judgments straight:** Charles C. Ryrie, *Revelation: Everyman's Bible Commentary* (Chicago, IL: Moody Publishers, 1996), 52-54.

349 **6+1=7:** E.W. Bullinger, "The Spiritual Significance of Numbers," *The Companion Bible:* Appendix 10 (Grand Rapids, MI: Kregel Publications, 1990), 14. A full treatment of the spiritual significance of numbers in scripture can be found in Bullinger's *Number in Scripture.*

Acknowledgments

The **frameworks** project began a few years ago during a time when I had limited my Bible teaching to adult New Testament Survey courses at various Bay Area churches. Being a visual learner myself, I tried my best to supplement my course material with charts, maps and drawings whenever possible.

One day, as I was fiddling around, trying to visualize New Testament book groups, I pulled out a magic marker and drew six boxes on a piece of paper. I made the width of each box represent the number of books in each group. To provide further clues as to what this drawing might mean, I placed numbers inside the boxes and slapped the title, **frameworks**, across the top.

Then, I left the house, drove to a local t-shirt shop and handed the owner my drawing. "Can you make me a long-sleeved black shirt with this drawing on the front?" "Yep," he said. I wore the shirt to my next class.

After everyone was seated, I pointed to the white, silkscreened boxes on my shirt and said, "What is this?" After a pregnant pause, someone guessed, "a software start-up," another, "a phone number?" "Do the math," I responded, "How many books in the New Testament?" Light bulbs went on all over the room. Soon, I had orders for 84 shirts. Not only had I created a new clothing line, I had started a cause.

Now, two years later, through the partnership of graphic designer, Bridget Whitaker, editors, Connie Pike, Jon Stoner and Andy Madsen and printing expert, Ron Meuser, that cause has blossomed into this book, dedicated to promoting biblical literacy everywhere in a fresh, visual way.

Special thanks to Doug Stevens for your advice and counsel and for pushing me to get it done, and to Costas Tsevas, for your unrivaled expertise in Greek language and biblical history.

Many thanks to Steve Madsen and Mark Calcagno at Cornerstone Fellowship, Scott Farmer and Terry Campbell at Community Presbyterian Church, and Morgan Murray and Bill and Roxie Herbert at Walnut Creek Presbyterian Church for sponsoring my courses over the years.

Thanks to all who invested in your own biblical literacy in classes at these great churches. Kudos to my remarkably loving, talented and dedicated Tuesday evening Bible Study group. You guys helped me give birth to this project, you believe in this cause and you continue to inspire me week after week.

Thanks also to our Focus Group and Beta Test team members, some who provided front-end design and content guidance, and others, advance copy reviews. Your comments, corrections and insights were invaluable: Jack and Karen Ables, Don Ankenbrandt, Bill Baggett, Cathy Burkholder, Kevin Carey, Judy Cimino, Sue Corsiglia, Michael Coutts, Joe DiPietro, Paul Dugan, Kim Dunn, Gail Gilpin, Sharon Grimshaw, Josh Hall, Andy and Tina Halvorsen, John Harkin, Howard Jarrell, Charlie Johnson, Lorene Johnson, Albert Lee, Kevin Madsen, Keri McCormick, Don and Jane Meek, BethAnn Moitoso, Heather Muncy, Dave Shields, Chris Stockhaus, Adrian Tsingaris, Carolin Wood, Michael Wood, Bob Wyckoff and Mike Yantis. Thanks to Linda Toqe for expert proofing.

Finally, thanks to family members, whose encouragement, support (and reviews), have been much appreciated. Thanks, Mom. Thanks, Kris and Chuck, Susanne, Greg and Hil. Thanks, Jon and Debbie, Joseph and Yasimine. Thanks, Laurel. Thanks Fred and Marilyn, Colette and Lonnie.

Special thanks to my wife, Bonnie, and to our tribe: Eric, Jayn, Chris, Ben, Peter and Jenna. This one's for you. And a special tribute to Gordon, Don and Dorothy, parents who left us before seeing the fruit of this labor.

Photo Credits